THE
CREATIVE WRITER

LEVEL ONE

FIVE FINGER EXERCISES

by

BORIS FISHMAN

Cover design by Sarah Park.

Publisher's Cataloging-In-Publication Data
(Prepared by The Donohue Group, Inc.)

Fishman, Boris, 1979-
   The creative writer. Level one, Five finger exercises / Boris
Fishman.

     p. : ill. ;   cm.

   Interest grade level: 5-8.
   "... designed to be used in a mentor/student relationship, with
teaching, guidance, and evaluation tips provided for the mentor or
teacher."--Publisher's e-mail communication.
   Includes index.
   ISBN: 978-1-933339-55-9

   1. Creative writing (Elementary education) 2. English language-
-Composition and exercises--Study and teaching (Elementary)
I. Title. II. Title: Five finger exercises

LB1576 .F57 2011
372.62/3
2011933500

The illustration on page 123 and on the back cover, Mark Rothko,
Untitled (Black on Gray), 1969/1970 Acrylic on canvas 80 1/8 x
69 1/8 inches (203.3 x 175.5 cm) is reproduced by permission of
Solomon R. Guggenheim Museum, New York Gift, The Mark Rothko
Foundation, Inc., 1986

DEDICATION

To Susan Wise Bauer, who provides an example.

HOW TO USE THIS BOOK

This book consists of 36 weeks of lessons and exercises, divided evenly into two sections: **Fiction** and **Poetry**. These, in turn, are divided into multi-week units of study such as Plot (in Fiction), Sound (in Poetry), and so on. The Fiction and Poetry sections culminate in assignments to write a complete short story and poem, respectively.

Although the first 18 weeks are devoted to fiction and the second 18 to poetry, all writers are encouraged to complete *both* sections. Awareness of plot and character makes for a better poet; understanding of meter and rhyme, a better fiction writer.

Each lesson is built around an exercise meant to practice that week's subject. In addition to the main exercise, each lesson provides challenge exercises for the writer willing to go further.

The Creative Writer provides an aspiring **writer** with a workshop-between-two-covers. Writing is an intensely individual undertaking, but it also must be practiced in relationship to others. Instead of merely addressing the writer, *The Creative Writer* also provides directions, instructions, and answers for a writing **mentor**. These mentoring sections, found at the end of the Fiction and Poetry assignments, allow any intelligent reader to help the aspiring writer—and recognize that writing is, ultimately, an act of **communication** with others.

Younger writers may give these mentor instructions to a parent or teacher; older writers, a trusted friend or colleague.

Those practicing on their own should feel free to look at the mentor guidance for useful tips on how to do the assigned exercises. Ultimately, though, the mentor sections should encourage solitary writers to find a writing community—and become part of it.

Introduction

To the Writer

So you want to write stories or poems (or both). Perhaps this is a new idea. Or maybe you've been writing for years. How will this book help make you a better writer?

Let's start by talking about what creative writing is. Creative writing tends to rely on the imagination much more than other kinds of writing. Also, creative writers pay attention not only to what a sentence says—that is, the information included in it—but also to *how* the sentence says it. Another way to put this would be: Creative writing pays attention not only to content but style.

Look at the following excerpt from an essay called "The Sands of Cape Cod" by the great American nature writer, Henry David Thoreau.

"The Sands of Cape Cod" by Henry David Thoreau

…The sand is the great enemy here. The tops of some of the hills were inclosed and a board put up forbidding all persons entering the inclosure, lest their feet should disturb the sand, and set it a-blowing or a-sliding. The sand drifts like snow, and sometimes the lower story of a house is concealed by it, though it is kept off by a wall. The houses were formerly built on piles, in order that the driving sand might pass under them. We saw a few old ones here still standing on their piles, but they were boarded up now, being protected by their younger neighbors. There was a schoolhouse, just under the hill on which we sat, filled with sand up to the tops of the desks, and of course the master and scholars had fled. Perhaps they had imprudently left the windows open one day, or neglected to mend a broken pane.[1]

---

1. From *Stories of Nature,* ed. Eva March Tappan (Macmillan, 1916), p. 489-90.

Note where Thoreau says "Sand is the great enemy here." Think about the images, feelings, and associations that phrasing brings up for you, as the reader. For me, it conjures sand as a marauding menace. Cape Cod is surrounded by water, so the sand is like some terrible, merciless invader storming the area from some faraway place.

Now imagine if Thoreau had written, "Sand is a big problem in Cape Cod." That gives you the same information, but would you agree that it comes across much less vividly? No colorful associations ("enemy") pop into the mind, no feelings are aroused ("problem" is mild; "enemy" is forceful); the brain sluggishly registers the information and stalls, waiting for more input instead of running off on an imaginative journey.

When we read writing that is vivid and original—because the author has chosen interesting and unusual words, images, or comparisons—we become more excited about what we're reading. Creative writers can spend an hour looking for the perfect word. Compare the verbs "throw," "chuck," and "lob." All more or less mean the same thing, right? But if you spend a bit more time thinking about each, you'll begin to notice subtle differences: "Throw" is generic, as generic as "Sand is a big problem." It does little more than communicate basic information. A "lob" is a specific kind of throw, a high arc. "Chuck," as in "He chucked the basketball," suggests casualness, disinterest, even derision. We chuck things about when we don't need—or want—to be careful. You couldn't get simple old "throw" to do that much suggestive work. You'd have to say, "He threw the basketball with irritation." This sentence is okay, but it's twice as long. And when sentence after sentence isn't as concise and efficient as it can be—when it uses more time to say something than it should—we become tired, just as we do with a person who says too much to make a simple point. Creative writers search for the perfect word because they want to say as much as they can with a single word or image. They want to keep the attention of their audience.

Creative writing doesn't only convey information; creative writing also **tells a story**. Compare these two sentences:

1. The train stalled between Washington and Richmond.
2. The train stalled between Washington and Richmond, making it almost certain that Sandra Hayes would miss the most important deadline of her life.

Which sentence is more likely to make you want to read on? I would guess the second. It's all well and good that the train has stalled, but Sandra Hayes might miss the most important deadline of her life! The deadline for what? What does she stand to lose if she doesn't make it? Note that I've gone even further to stir up suspense in the second sentence by saying "making it *almost certain*" that she would miss the deadline. This keeps both options open and ratchets up the suspense. Imagine if I'd written "The train stalled between Washington and Richmond, making Sandra Hayes miss the most important deadline of her life." The most-important-deadline stuff is still intriguing, but we're no longer so close to the edge of our seats. Sandra's missed it already; what can she do? Next time you watch a movie, or read a book, try to pay attention to what gets you excited to keep watching and reading in this way. Such details make us want to see films, read books, and follow narrative in general, whether on a weekly TV show or in a children's book series.

One other note about the sentences above: Both of them situate us in concrete places (Washington, Richmond) and give us specific details about what's happening (train, stalling). This helps readers imagine the scene. Let's create a different comparison using only the first sentence:

1. The train stalled.
2. The train stalled between Washington and Richmond.

Isn't the second option more engaging? Why? It's because we've been given concrete details; we can imagine Washington and the countryside outside it, which is probably lush and green. Same goes for Richmond. (We'd imagine something very different if the train had stalled between Calgary and Vancouver.) Being able to place the reader in the moment helps involve her in a story, helps make her care about what's going to happen.

And, while we're here, note the particularity of the verb "stall." Imagine how differently we would react if the sentence said something more generic, such as "got stuck," or worse, "stopped moving." "Stall" is more particular to vehicles, and, therefore, makes what's going on much easier to imagine for the reader. "Stall" means that something with the mechanism went awry; "stopped moving" could be the result of 10 different things, which frustrates the reader with its vagueness.

An understanding of some of the things I've mentioned above can help writers improve dramatically. We're going to get into all of them, some in this year's course, some in future levels of this series. By practicing what's known as craft, you will make your writing more original, memorable, and interesting. But this course alone will take you only part of the way. Exercises and writing practice are only some of the components of the balanced creative diet that will make you a much better writer.

What else should you be doing?

1. **Reading.** Read every day. As you go through this and future levels of this series, you will begin reading stories and books as a writer, not just as a reader. You will see behind the curtain of the finished, published lines and understand how the author-magician came up with these particular words and ideas, and why. Reading for information or entertainment is passive, like watching television. As a writer, you must read actively. Pay attention to the author's word choices. Think about why the author decided to have this character do that at this point in the story. And so on.

Most of the lessons in this book are followed by challenge exercises. Here's a book-wide challenge exercise: Every time you learn about a new craft skill in this course, try to explore it in your reading outside the course.

2. **Writing.** The exercises in this course will give you a great way to practice your writing skills, but you must continue to write stories and poems outside of this course as well.

3. **Keeping an observation notebook.** I'd like you to get in the habit of carrying a little notebook and pencil wherever you go. Inspiration doesn't strike only when we're at our desks, ready to write. It usually strikes at less convenient times—when we're playing in the park, standing in line at the grocery store, running the dog. As you go through the lessons in this book, you'll begin to develop an eye and ear for all kinds of things that slipped by you before. You will want to jot them down. You need a notebook to do that. If you wait until you get home to write them down, chances are you will have forgotten. The best writers always have an observation notebook handy.

A great deal of your training as a writer will occur away from your writing desk. Writers write about the world around them, so they pay attention to that world all the time: to the way people speak, to what makes them laugh or worry, to other small details. Not even a memory champion will remember all of this once seated at the writing desk. That's why you need your notebook. As the great American novelist Philip Roth has written, "You must not forget anything."

Introduction

To the Mentor

Teaching creative writing is tricky. Some respected writers look down on the very idea. They make two arguments: 1) You can't teach talent; 2) Teaching craft—point of view, character, dialogue, etc.—results in cookie-cutter work. Better to let the writer roam more or less aimlessly, discovering her gift—if she has one, of course—along the way.

I wouldn't disagree in full. Talent *can't* be taught. And it *is* true that, with the spread of MFA programs, we're seeing a lot of graduates with technical aptitude but little artistic distinction.

But I disagree with the explore-without-guidance idea. I did it, for years, as a young writer. Two years in an MFA program did far more for me in far less time. There, I encountered in organized form, presented by writers with decades of practice, the insights into character, plot, etc. that I had been trying to divine more or less by instinct. I didn't adopt their lessons indiscriminately. Some made sense, others didn't, still others served as a springboard that brought me to new ideas, and by far the largest number went into a kind of reserve, deployable on a case-by-case basis. But I left a far wiser writer.

In particular, poetry instruction books for young writers tend to avoid craft guidance, perhaps because they regard it as too complicated. Instead, they direct young poets, lesson after lesson, to practice writing poems on new subjects: last night's dream; what you would do if you were a bird. This kind of imaginative work can get new writers excited about writing, but in focusing mostly on subject matter, it does little to teach the beginner *how* to write a poem. *The Creative Writer* tries to lay the foundation for a lifetime of creative work by teaching the *how*: the skills of writing, observation, feeling, discipline, analysis, planning, revision, etc. that make the best writers. It may be tough for the writer to appreciate at this point *why*, say, revision leads to better work—I discuss such rationales more in the mentor guidance—but it's still valuable to guide him through the revision of a story.

Craft

None of the craft concepts discussed in this course require a PhD or run against instinct. In fact, we already possess many of the skills of observation and writing they refer to. This course simply aims to make the writer more *conscious* of them, so they can be deployed judiciously. Used properly, craft can be the key that unlocks a writer's potential. It should be a handmaiden to artistic instinct, not a replacement for it. Without craft, the genius writer may emerge with a bracing, visionary work, but I think this is likely for one writer out of a thousand. For the rest of us, some of whom possess talent, avoidance of craft education is likely to lead to a story like so many of the kind I produced as an undergraduate: an unwieldy, bloated mess with some potential concealed underneath.

Craft taught me how to rein in some impulses while setting others free. It has helped recalibrate my fiction from the unedited outpourings of a sensitive soul to what a wise person has called "disciplined abandon"—premeditated, controlled, shaped drama. (There's a romantic idea out there that writers are mediums, channeling a gift of divine inspiration, but this couldn't be further from the truth. The best writers are cabinetmakers. There are plenty of moments of unscheduled inspiration, but most of a novel or book of poetry emerges from day after day in a chair, many of them spent staring at a blank page and thinking, feeling, crafting.) Once we learn more about craft, we can decide when to follow the guidance and when to ignore it. But before the rules can be broken, they have to be learned.

All this is especially true for young writers. The lessons in this book will give them a post to hang on to as they brave the monsoon of a blank page. Nothing is more terrifying than that blank page, even to writers who've written half a dozen books. In a young writer, it can lead to creative paralysis. (The idea of starting a new novel, having just finished one, puts me in a cold sweat.) And even if your child has been scribbling stories without a burp of self-consciousness since the age of 2, these exercises can help her shape those stories into something greater.

Generally, even if your writer does not end up becoming a poet or novelist, the skills she will learn in this book will make her more expressive, more observant of and empathetic with the world around her, and wiser as a human being. It will give her skills that will be of use in whatever profession she chooses. The skills of creative writing are essential for anyone wishing to write a lucid, compelling legal brief; a promotional advertisement that stands out from the usual eye-glazing drone of marketing materials; or, for that matter, a college paper. (Put yourself in the shoes of those professors—they've been reading dozens of papers a week for years, if not decades, and react very gratefully to stuff that feels fresh.) Vivid, concise writing is one of the most elusive skills in the modern workplace, and one of the most critical. This course will make your child better at it—and maybe you, too.

Table of Contents

Part I: <u>Fiction</u>

Part II: <u>Poetry</u>

PART I

FICTION

Section 1:
Plot

Weeks 1–4

Week 1

Plot points

Purpose: To understand how stories come together.

Plot, simply, is what happens in a story. Every time something new and significant happens in a story, that's a plot point. Don't think of plot points too scientifically. Have you ever told a story? Every time you said "and then," you were moving on to a new plot point.

A very brief version of the plot of *Alice in Wonderland* is: A girl falls down a rabbit hole and meets all sorts of strange creatures. A larger version of the plot would include a lot more detail.

This week, we're going to acquaint ourselves with plot by looking closely at a published story. Think of your task as dismantling a watch to see how all the pieces fit together to make it tick: You'll be taking a finished story apart into its pieces to help you understand how it works, and you'll accomplish this by finding the major plot points in the story.

Let me give you an example by showing you the major plot points in a scene from *The Adventures of Tom Sawyer*. Then, I'll ask you to read the fairy tale "Rapunzel" by the Brothers Grimm and find that story's plot points in the same way.

Read the following excerpt from *The Adventures of Tom Sawyer,* by Mark Twain.

> Monday morning found Tom Sawyer miserable. Monday morning always found him so—because it began another week's slow suffering in school. He generally began that day with wishing he had had no intervening holiday, it made the going into captivity and fetters again so much more odious.
>
> Tom lay thinking. Presently it occurred to him that he wished he was sick; then he could stay home from school. Here was a vague possibility. He canvassed his system.

Boris Fishman

No ailment was found, and he investigated again. This time he thought he could detect colicky symptoms, and he began to encourage them with considerable hope. But they soon grew feeble, and presently died wholly away. He reflected further. Suddenly he discovered something. One of his upper front teeth was loose. This was lucky; he was about to begin to groan, as a "starter," as he called it, when it occurred to him that if he came into court with that argument, his aunt would pull it out, and that would hurt. So he thought he would hold the tooth in reserve for the present, and seek further. Nothing offered for some little time, and then he remembered hearing the doctor tell about a certain thing that laid up a patient for two or three weeks and threatened to make him lose a finger. So the boy eagerly drew his sore toe from under the sheet and held it up for inspection. But now he did not know the necessary symptoms. However, it seemed well worth while to chance it, so he fell to groaning with considerable spirit.

But Sid slept on unconscious.

Tom groaned louder, and fancied that he began to feel pain in the toe.

No result from Sid.

Tom was panting with his exertions by this time. He took a rest and then swelled himself up and fetched a succession of admirable groans.

Sid snored on.

Tom was aggravated. He said, "Sid, Sid!" and shook him. This course worked well, and Tom began to groan again. Sid yawned, stretched, then brought himself up on his elbow with a snort, and began to stare at Tom. Tom went on groaning. Sid said:

"Tom! Say, Tom!" [No response.] "Here, Tom! TOM! What is the matter, Tom?" And he shook him and looked in his face anxiously.

Tom moaned out: "Oh, don't, Sid. Don't joggle me."

"Why, what's the matter, Tom? I must call auntie."

"No—never mind. It'll be over by and by, maybe. Don't call anybody."

"But I must! DON'T groan so, Tom, it's awful. How long you been this way?"

"Hours. Ouch! Oh, don't stir so, Sid, you'll kill me."

"Tom, why didn't you wake me sooner? Oh, Tom, DON'T! It makes my flesh crawl to hear you. Tom, what is the matter?"

"I forgive you everything, Sid. [Groan.] Everything you've ever done to me. When I'm gone—"

"Oh, Tom, you ain't dying, are you? Don't, Tom—oh, don't. Maybe—"

"I forgive everybody, Sid. [Groan.] Tell 'em so, Sid. And Sid, you give my window-sash and my cat with one eye to that new girl that's come to town, and tell her—"

But Sid had snatched his clothes and gone. Tom was suffering in reality, now, so handsomely was his imagination working, and so his groans had gathered quite a genuine tone.

Sid flew down-stairs and said: "Oh, Aunt Polly, come! Tom's dying!"

"Dying!"

"Yes'm. Don't wait—come quick!"

"Rubbage! I don't believe it!"

But she fled up-stairs, nevertheless, with Sid and Mary at her heels. And her face grew white, too, and her lip trembled. When she reached the bedside she gasped out:

"You, Tom! Tom, what's the matter with you?"

"Oh, auntie, I'm—"

"What's the matter with you—what is the matter with you, child?"

"Oh, auntie, my sore toe's mortified!"

The old lady sank down into a chair and laughed a little, then cried a little, then did both together. This restored her and she said: "Tom, what a turn you did give me. Now you shut up that nonsense and climb out of this."

The groans ceased and the pain vanished from the toe. The boy felt a little foolish, and he said: "Aunt Polly, it SEEMED mortified, and it hurt so I never minded my tooth at all."

"Your tooth, indeed! What's the matter with your tooth?"

"One of them's loose, and it aches perfectly awful."

"There, there, now, don't begin that groaning again. Open your mouth. Well—your tooth IS loose, but you're not going to die about that. Mary, get me a silk thread, and a chunk of fire out of the kitchen."

Tom said: "Oh, please, auntie, don't pull it out. It don't hurt any more. I wish I may never stir if it does. Please don't, auntie. I don't want to stay home from school."

"Oh, you don't, don't you? So all this row was because you thought you'd get to stay home from school and go a-fishing? Tom, Tom, I love you so, and you seem to try every way you can to break my old heart with your outrageousness." By this time the dental instruments were ready. The old lady made one end of the silk thread fast to Tom's tooth with a loop and tied the other to the bedpost. Then she seized the chunk of fire and suddenly thrust it almost into the boy's face. The tooth hung dangling by the bedpost, now.

But all trials bring their compensations. As Tom wended to school after breakfast, he was the envy of every boy he met because the gap in his upper row of teeth enabled him to expectorate in a new and admirable way. He gathered quite a following of lads interested in the exhibition; and one that had cut his finger and had been a centre of fascination and homage up to this time, now found himself suddenly without an adherent, and shorn of his glory. His heart was heavy, and he said with a disdain which he did not feel that it wasn't anything to spit like Tom Sawyer; but another boy said, "Sour grapes!" and he wandered away a dismantled hero.[2]

---

2. From *The Adventures of Tom Sawyer*, by Mark Twain (CreateSpace, 2010), pp. 37–39.

Since I will ask you to come up with 10 plot points for "Rapunzel," here's a 10-point **plot summary** of this snippet from *Tom Sawyer*:

1. Tom searched himself for aches that could keep him out of school.
2. He found a loose tooth but decided against using it as the excuse.
3. Then he found pain in his toe.
4. He started groaning very loudly, hoping to get Sid's attention.
5. Sid awoke and, seeing Tom wailing with agony, ran downstairs to get Aunt Polly.
6. Aunt Polly figured out pretty quickly that nothing serious was wrong.
7. Tom resorted to Plan B: the tooth.
8. Against Tom's pleas, Aunt Polly pulled it out.
9. Tom went to school after all.
10. Unexpectedly, he was the source of attention because the new gap in his teeth allowed him to spit in new and creative ways.

In the above, note that I didn't go into too much detail—I hit just the basics. Two good guidelines for plot summaries:

• Try to write it so that someone reading only the plot summary could get a pretty good idea of what the story's about, without any major blank spots. The opposite of this is true, too: If the summary makes sense without a piece of information, you can leave it out. For instance: Is it crucial for someone reading the summary to know that Tom was trying to get out of school? Yes. Is it crucial for this person to know that Mondays always put Tom in a funk? Not as much.

• Try to make room for information that will be necessary later on. For instance, #9 wouldn't make much sense without #1. And #7 wouldn't make much sense without #2.

Your turn. Read the fairy tale below and list its 10 main plot points, using the guidelines above. If you can write them down from memory after you finish the story, that's great. But if you'd like to help yourself as you read, you can put a checkmark in the margin every time something "new" happens. When you're done reading, you can go back to your checkmarks and use the plot points they refer to as your 10. Either way, a good way to guide yourself, after you've written down the first plot point in your summary, is to ask: "What happened next?"

Before you start, you might want to know that "rampion" is a kind of flower with an edible root that resembles turnip. It's often used in salads in Europe. An "ell" is the length of a man's arm. (Whenever you encounter words whose definitions you don't know, make a point of looking them up in a dictionary. In fact, you should devote a portion of your practice notebook to vocabulary. By the time you're done with this course, you may have quite a list of newly learned words.)

"Rapunzel"
by the Brothers Grimm

THERE was once a man and a woman who had long in vain wished for a child. At length the woman hoped that God was about to grant her desire. These people had a little window at the back of their house from which a splendid garden could be seen, which was full of the most beautiful flowers and herbs. It was, however, surrounded by a high wall, and no one dared to go into it because it belonged to an enchantress, who had great power and was dreaded by all the world.

One day the woman was standing by this window and looking down into the garden, when she saw a bed which was planted with the most beautiful rampion (rapunzel), and it looked so fresh and green that she longed for it, and had the greatest desire to eat some. This desire increased every day, and as she knew that she could not get any of it, she quite pined away, and looked pale and miserable. Then her husband was alarmed, and asked, "What ails you, dear wife?" "Ah," she replied, "if I can't get some of the rampion, which is in the garden behind our house, to eat, I shall die."

The man, who loved her, thought, "Sooner than let your wife die, bring her some of the rampion yourself, let it cost you what it will." In the twilight of evening, he clambered down over the wall into the garden of the enchantress, hastily clutched a handful of rampion, and took it to his wife. She at once made herself a salad of it, and ate it with much relish. She, however, liked it so much—so very much—that the next day she longed for it three times as much as before. If he was to have any rest, her husband must once more descend into the garden. In the gloom of evening, therefore, he let himself down again; but when he had clambered down the wall he was terribly afraid, for he saw the enchantress standing before him.

"How can you dare," said she with angry look, "to descend into my garden and steal my rampion like a thief? You shall suffer for it!"

"Ah," answered he, "let mercy take the place of justice, I only made up my mind to do it out of necessity. My wife saw your rampion from the window, and felt such a longing for it that she would have died if she had not got some to eat."

Then the enchantress allowed her anger to be softened, and said to him, "If the case be as you say, I will allow you to take away with you as much rampion as you will, only I make one condition. You must give me the child which your wife will bring into the world; it shall be well treated, and I will care for it like a mother." The man in his terror consented to everything, and when the woman gave birth, the enchantress appeared at once, gave the child the name of Rapunzel, and took it away with her.

Rapunzel grew into the most beautiful child beneath the sun. When she was twelve years old, the enchantress shut her into a tower, which lay in a forest, and had neither stairs nor door, but quite at the top was a little window. When the enchantress wanted to go in, she placed herself beneath this and cried,

"Rapunzel, Rapunzel, Let down your hair to me."

Rapunzel had magnificent long hair, fine as spun gold, and when she heard the voice of the enchantress she unfastened her braided tresses, wound them round one of the hooks of the window above, and then the hair fell twenty ells down, and the enchantress climbed up by it.

After a year or two, it came to pass that the King's son rode through the forest and went by the tower. Then he heard a song, which was so charming that he stood still and listened. This was Rapunzel, who in her solitude passed her time in letting her sweet voice resound. The King's son wanted to climb up to her, and looked for the door of the tower, but none was to be found. He rode home, but the singing had so deeply touched his heart, that every day he went out into the forest and listened to it. Once when he was thus standing behind a tree, he saw that an enchantress came there, and he heard how she cried,

"Rapunzel, Rapunzel, Let down your hair."

Then Rapunzel let down the braids of her hair, and the enchantress climbed up to her. "If that is the ladder by which one mounts, I will for once try my fortune," said he, and the next day when it began to grow dark, he went to the tower and cried,

"Rapunzel, Rapunzel, Let down thy hair."

Immediately the hair fell down and the King's son climbed up.

At first Rapunzel was terribly frightened when a man such as her eyes had never yet beheld, came to her; but the King's son began to talk to her quite like a friend, and told her that his heart had been so stirred that it had let him have no rest, and he had been forced to see her. Then Rapunzel lost her fear, and when he asked her if she would take him for her husband, and she saw that he was young and handsome, she thought, "He will love me more than old Dame Gothel [the enchantress] does;" and she said yes, and laid her hand in his. She said, "I will willingly go away with you, but I do not know how to get down. Bring with you a skein of silk every time that you come, and I will weave a ladder with it, and when that is ready I will descend, and you will take me on the horse."

They agreed that until that time he should come to her every evening, for the old woman came by day. The enchantress remarked nothing of this, until once Rapunzel said to her, "Tell me, Dame Gothel, how it happens that you are so much heavier for me to draw up than the young King's son—he is with me in a moment."

"Ah! you wicked child," cried the enchantress, "What do I hear you say! I thought I had separated you from all the world, and yet you have deceived me!" In her anger she clutched Rapunzel's beautiful tresses, wrapped them twice round her left hand, seized a pair of scissors with the right, and snip, snap, they were cut off, and the lovely braids lay on the ground. And she was so pitiless that she took poor Rapunzel into a desert where she had to live in great grief and misery.

On the same day, however, that she cast out Rapunzel, the enchantress in the evening fastened the braids of hair which she had cut off to the hook of the window, and when the King's son came and cried, "Rapunzel, Rapunzel, Let down your hair," she let the hair down. The King's son ascended, but he did not find his dearest Rapunzel above, but the enchantress, who gazed at him with wicked and venomous looks. "Aha!" she cried mockingly, "You would fetch your dearest, but the beautiful bird sits no longer singing in the nest; the cat has got it, and will scratch out your eyes as well. Rapunzel is lost to you; you will never see her more."

The King's son was beside himself with pain, and in his despair he leapt down from the tower. He escaped with his life, but the thorns into which he fell pierced his eyes. Then he wandered quite blind about the forest, ate nothing but roots and berries, and did nothing but lament and weep over the loss of his dearest wife. Thus he roamed about in misery for some years, and at length came to the desert where Rapunzel lived in wretchedness. He heard a voice, and it seemed so familiar to him that he went towards it, and when he approached, Rapunzel knew him and fell on his neck and wept. Two of her tears wetted his eyes and they grew clear again, and he could see with them as before. He led her to his kingdom where he was joyfully received, and they lived for a long time afterwards, happy and contented. [3]

---

3.   From "Grimm's Tales" in *The Harvard Classics*, Vol. 17, ed. by Charles William Eliot (New York, 1909), pp. 71–74.

Each of your plot points should be about a sentence long. If you're squeezing too much into a single sentence, you can break up the information into two sentences.

Plot:

1. _____

2. _____

3. _____

4. _____

5. _____

6. _____

7. _____

8. _____

9. _____

10. _____

After you've finished, spend some time rereading your plot points. This list is the plot of the story broken down to its essentials. Like the beams of a house visible during construction, it exhibits the basic structural framework that holds the building of the story together and keeps readers excited to find out what happens next. The authors may have come up with the entire story plan in advance, or they may have gotten an idea for how to start and then improvised from there as they went. Either way, try to understand that a story isn't pulled out of thin air. It takes forethought and an awareness of what will keep the reader's attention.

Challenge exercises:

1. Not only books have plot. So do movies, plays, sometimes even dance numbers. Pick a favorite movie and write a 10-point plot summary for it.

2. In your 10-point plot summary for "Rapunzel," cross out numbers 6–10 and come up with five new plot points—a new, invented ending for the story.

Week 2

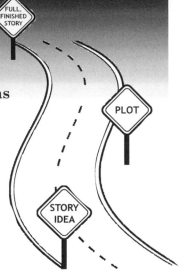

Come up with 10 story ideas

Purpose: To practice coming up with the essential building block of a story—the story idea.

Last week, you took a finished story apart into its plot points. Before you can have plot points, you need a plot, or a general idea of what the story will be about. Think of these as way stations on a Story Road that begins with Story Idea (A), continues to Plot Points (B), and ends with a Full, Finished Story (C). In Week 1, you went from C to B. This week, we'll be practicing A.

What makes a good story idea? There are some very complex answers to this question, but a very simple one will do for the time being: anything that makes a reader want to read on. Sometimes, we can't put a story down because we fall in love with a character. Sometimes, it's because the author is very funny or writes beautifully. When we can't put down a story because of its plot, that's because we're dying to find out what happens next. That could be because the author has described to us a conflict between two parties and we want to find out which one will get the upper hand. Or it's because we've met a character who really, really wants something, and because we're interested in this character, we'd like to find out if he or she is going to get it. In the words of a young writer I know, "All you need for a good story is characters you care about and the problem they're going to solve." Whether they're going to solve it is what keeps us reading. This is called "suspense."

So, suspense might be one element of a good plot. The occurrence of something unusual might be another. Think about it: A typical day in your home might not make for an exciting short story. But what about a day that begins like any other day but ends with an appearance by a mysterious visitor, a man in a black trench coat and top hat who claims to have known your father in college—and can quote random tidbits about what he was like there—but whom your father doesn't remember at all... .

This week, you will come up with 10 story ideas of your own.

In coming up with the 10 story ideas, try to describe situations likely to make your readers curious to read on. If you're stuck, pick the nearest object or person and ask yourself two questions: What type of out-of-the-ordinary thing might happen to this person or object? Or: How can I create suspense using this object?

Here's an example of the first: Are you sitting in the kitchen right now? Is there a toaster? What if... the toaster stops requiring electricity in order to function? What if—continuing with this thought—the oven starts cooking dinner without having to be turned on? What if the household appliances start developing personalities and start being able to move? Maybe the washing machine rumbles out of its place in the garage, bumps around the house collecting everyone's laundry, and washes it without needing to be turned on. Maybe it does this even though the laundry doesn't have to be done. Maybe no one can leave the house because the washing machine has taken everyone's clothes hostage! And so on. As you can see, a very simple starting point like a toaster can take us to very exciting and unusual places.

Here's an example of the second: You might be sitting at your kitchen table and looking at your brother as he prepares for guitar practice. Maybe he likes a girl in town, and because he knows she likes music, he recently took up guitar. His band is in the final round of a town-wide Battle of the Bands competition against a band featuring a popular kid who's been playing guitar his whole life. Maybe his dad was a guitarist in a famous rock band! Maybe the kid got lessons from Paul McCartney of the Beatles! Wouldn't we want to know who won this competition?

Here are several more examples of story ideas:

1. The last time you were scared: What was making you scared? How did the situation resolve itself?

2. Your mom comes home one day and acts the opposite of her usual self. Nothing obviously spooky happens—she doesn't grow fangs or begin to fly around on black wings—but you start feeling a sneaky suspicion that she's not herself.

3. Someone you know has the opportunity to get a lot of money if he cheats. What does he do? And what's the situation?

4. A rancher has had his prize bull killed and sets off to find the attacker. What happens?

These story ideas all have a question whose answer the author is hoping his readers will want to find out.

In #1, what's making the narrator scared and how will he defeat the fear?

In #2, what's really going on with the narrator's mom?

In #3, does the person cheat, and what are the consequences?

In #4, does the rancher find the person who killed his bull?

Your turn. The situation you describe can be as brief as a sentence or as long as a paragraph. Like the story ideas above, your situation should feature some kind of question or mystery likely to make a reader want to read on.

1. _____

2. _____

3. _____

4. _____

5. _____

6. _____

7. _____

8. _____

9. _____

10. _____

Challenge exercise:

In one sentence—no more than 25 words—write out the story idea behind your favorite movie. Do the same thing for your favorite book.

Week 3

Turn a photograph into a story

Purpose: To come up with a plot using the image in a photograph.

This exercise will test your story-inventing skills. Find a photograph, preferably with no caption and no clues to what's in it. A photograph of a man looking to the side in excitement (we can't see what he's excited about) is better than a photograph of a row of chocolates in a chocolate shop. The latter example is just business as usual—a chocolate shop is selling chocolates. (Though you're welcome to imagine an unusual and surprising story around those chocolates.) I'm just saying that it's easier for the imagination to start running if there's a ready mystery in the photograph: Whose hand is that? Why is the man crying? Why is that man excited? And so on.

You can look for a photograph online, in an old book, or in a current magazine. Take at least a half-hour to find a good one. How do you know you've found a good one? That's the one that puzzles you, makes you wonder about what's going on in the photo, or catches your attention so that you forget you're looking for a photograph for an assignment.

Then write 500 words in narrative form about the photograph. ("Narrative form" means that you would write it like a diary entry, one sentence following the next. The alternative would be to jot down observations in your notebook where each new observation is a bullet point, beginning a new line.) Imagine you're explaining what's going on in the photograph to someone who can't see it. Don't limit yourself to what you can see; imagine as much detail outside the photograph as you can. Here are some potential questions to answer:

1. What do we see in the photograph?

2. What do we not see in the photograph, but know must be near?

3. Are there people, or parts of people, in the photograph?

4. What kind of mood are they in?

5. Let's guess who they are based on how they're dressed or what they're doing.

6. What happened to these people yesterday?

7. What do they hope will happen tomorrow?

8. What is their relationship to one another?

And so on. (Remember: There are no incorrect answers.)

Feel free to devote more than one sentence to a particular detail of the photograph. In fact, if you wanted to devote your entire entry to a single thing about the photograph that caught your attention, feel free.

Challenge exercise:

Do you have a camera? Tell a story in 25 photographs using your camera. This will, of course, require you to think about what's going to happen in the story. If it's a story about a boy's dream of basketball stardom, you'll need your brother, a hoop, and... well, there are so many directions in which you could go. You may wish to write a "script"—a plan for the photographs— before you start, or you may want to be spontaneous. This assignment should remind you a little of your plot summary in Week 1. There, you practiced telling a story through an outline of the main plot points. You had to say a great deal in only 10 sentences. Here, you'll be summarizing a story in 25 photographs.

Week 4

Map out a story idea with plot points

Purpose: To take a story idea one step closer to being a finished story by plotting out, step by step, what will happen in the story.

In Week 1, you took a finished story (Station C on the Story Road) apart into its plot points (Station B). In Week 2, you practiced coming up with story ideas (Station A). This week, we're going to take some ideas for stories (A) and give them plot points (B).

You can have as many plot points as you'd like. Your mission is to describe what happens in this story, step by step, and if that takes more than the 10 entries we used in Week 2, that's fine. In length, they can be anywhere from a sentence to a paragraph.

How to do this? Let's use one of my story ideas from Week 2 as an example. Remember the story in which household appliances came to life? Here's what I wrote in Week 2:

Are you sitting in the kitchen right now? Is there a toaster? What if... the toaster stops requiring electricity in order to function? What if—continuing with this thought—the oven starts cooking dinner without having to be turned on? What if the household appliances start developing personalities and start being able to move? Maybe the washing machine rumbles out of its place in the garage, bumps around the house collecting everyone's laundry, and washes it without needing to be turned on. Maybe it does this even though the laundry doesn't have to be done. Maybe no one can leave the house because the washing machine has taken everyone's clothes hostage! And so on. As you can see, a very simple starting point like a toaster can take us to very exciting and unusual places.

You've got several plot points just in the description above:
1. The toaster stops requiring electricity in order to function.
2. The oven starts cooking dinner without having to be turned on.
3. The household appliances start developing personalities and start being able to move.

4. The washing machine rumbles out of its place in the garage, bumps around the house collecting everyone's laundry, and washes it without needing to be turned on.
5. Soon it starts doing laundry even though the laundry doesn't need doing.
6. No one can leave the house because the washing machine has taken everyone's clothes hostage!

As you can see, there's an escalation taking place here: First the toaster comes to life, then the oven, then the washing machine. At first, this is a positive development: How helpful that the washing machine collects and washes the laundry by itself! But then, the plot turns dark: The washing machine starts hijacking everyone's laundry. So we've got some suspense here: How is this problematic situation going to be resolved? That's what you'd have to figure out in the remainder of the plot points.

Creative writing textbooks have all kinds of formal names for what I described above: The escalation is known as *rising action*; the big moment of resolution—in this case, perhaps a confrontation between someone in your family and the leader of the appliances—is known as *climax*; the tying up of loose ends that happens afterward is called *falling action* or *resolution*; and so on. You don't have to concern yourself with these terms now; the more important thing is that you know them instinctively: A story has to have a beginning, a middle, and an end. Think of your favorite movie or book: We meet the characters, we learn about the situation in which they find themselves, we learn about what they want, and we read or watch on to find out how things turn out.

You could use one of the story ideas you came up with in Week 2. If you'd like to try something different, here are some other ideas:

1. Two sisters compete against each other in the finals of a sport. Tell us what sport, what kind of relationship they have, who wins, and how it happens.
2. Tell a story of how trapped miners kept up their spirits—or not—until they were rescued.
3. You're the owner of a basketball team down on its luck. It hasn't won in years and is out of money. A businessman from another town offers to buy the team, but that would mean its relocation from the town where it has been based for nearly 50 years, a town where everyone loves the team. What happens?
4. A boy runs away from home to find a wizard because he is looking for the answer to a question. What is the question? What happens in his quest?

Section 2: Character

Weeks 5–8

Week 5

Who is this character?

Purpose: To invent situations for real-life characters and imagine their behavior based on what you already know about them.

This week, we'll be shifting from plot to character. You can't have a story without something happening, and you can't have much happen without characters to whom it will happen.

This week's exercise will have two parts.

Part 1:

In a couple of weeks, I'll ask you to create a character from scratch, but for now, let's stick with characters whom we already know, whether from literature, movies, or real life. Do you have a beloved literary character—maybe the hero or heroine of your favorite novel? A favorite actor or movie character? Or maybe you're curious about someone in town, like the blind man who works in the ice cream store? (How *does* he read a book, or type on a computer, or make ice cream?) Or how about a sibling?

The first part of your assignment is to pick a character whom you already know and write 300 words describing what you know about him or her (or it). Try to go beyond facts like "has brown hair." Try to describe this person's behavior, and what it says about his or her personality. You may find it easier to do this in bullet-point form.

For instance, you might have noticed that the blind man at the ice cream store is very shy; or very talkative; or always has music playing, which none of the other employees do. You might have noticed that he likes rock 'n roll; that he has a long scar on his cheek; that he sits down on an upturned bucket every time things get slow. And so on. You may wish to spend some time observing the character you have in mind before making these notes.

Part 2:

For the second part of the exercise, describe an invented situation in which the character you've chosen appears. In other words, place someone you know in a situation in which you've never seen him or her, and tell us what happens. If we're sticking with the man at the ice cream store, you might imagine him witnessing a robbery. Or you might imagine him at home with his wife. Or you might imagine him watching a ballgame despite being blind. Whichever situation you come up with, spend 300 words describing to us—in narrative form—what is happening. If it's a robbery, tell us where we are, how the man determines a robbery is going on, how he reacts. If it's a ballgame at home, tell us how the man makes out the score, what he's doing while he's watching, what his house looks like in general. (As you'll learn in later weeks, you can reveal someone's character not only by saying things like "He was kind." For instance, if a character's home is very messy, doesn't that show something about him without the author having to say a word?)

Challenge exercise:

Take us through a day in the life of the character we've been talking about, from morning to night.

What are his morning habits?
What kind of car does he drive?
Does he have dinner early?
What are his pet peeves?

Describe for 300 words in narrative or bullet-point form.

Week 6

Historical characters

Purpose: To imagine new details about characters who really existed.

What are you studying in history right now? Your job this week will be to imagine yourself as a character in those events. For example, if you are reading about Columbus's discovery of America, you can imagine that you are a captain or sailor on one of Columbus's three ships, prowling for the riches of the Orient.

Write 300 words, either in narrative form or as bullet-point entries, telling us about you: What's your name? What do you look like? Are your teeth in good shape? Is there a family waiting for you back in…speaking of which, what country are you from? Spain, whose king and queen sent Columbus on this voyage, or Italy, like Columbus, or somewhere else? How did you end up on these Spanish ships? Do you think Columbus is an able leader? Do you think he will find the gold of Cathay?

You can write in **first-person** or **third-person point of view. Point of view** refers to the perspective from which you're telling the story. First-person means you're writing the story with yourself as the sailor ("I come from a small village in Italy…"). Third-person means you're writing *about* the sailor ("He comes from a small village in Italy…"). More on point of view in another lesson.

Try to imagine answers that would make sense in the context of what you're studying. For instance, could one of Columbus's sailors have read about the trip on the Internet? Of course not—this was 500 years ago! Could he have joined the crew because he had a cousin who had been on a previous expedition with Columbus and vouched for him? More likely. The idea of this exercise is to use your imagination to make history come alive, but also to use your mind to rein in your imagination when appropriate. (And don't worry too much about the facts of the story. For the purposes of this assignment, it doesn't matter how the sailor in question *really* learned about the voyage. Anything you make up will be fine.)

If no historical character jumps out at you, let's play a game. Name five events or historical periods in history. If you're stuck, what about:

1. The first modern Olympics in 1896 in Athens, Greece
2. The sinking of the Titanic
3. The building of the Great Wall of China
4. Alexander the Great's conquests
5. World War II

Now, list one character from each event or period, famous or not, young or old, male or female:

1. A person carrying the Olympic torch
2. A man traveling to meet his beloved
3. The architect of the Wall
4. A foot soldier
5. Winston Churchill

Finally, come up with five context-appropriate questions for each of these characters:

For #1, the person carrying the famous Olympic torch:
How was he chosen for this duty? Is he from Greece or another country? What is he wearing? Etc.

For #2, the man traveling to meet his beloved:
Are they meeting for the first time; that is, is it an arranged marriage? What does he do? Where does she live? Etc.

And so on.

After this exercise, you should have more than a handful of characters with lives to imagine.

Week 7

Heroes and villains

Purpose: To figure out why we like some characters and dislike others.

Think of the last book you read or movie you watched. Was there a character you were rooting for or against? Didn't your feelings about this character make you care more about the outcome of the story? The best books make us forget that we're reading fiction. We slip into a kind of dream—in the back of our minds, we know the events on the page are not true, but we're so engrossed in what's happening, it might as well be real. Characters play a very important role in this "illusion"—we root for or against them as if we were part of the story ourselves. (Just imagine the opposite: a book or movie with no characters at all. Wouldn't that be pretty boring, not to mention unrealistic?)

To begin to understand how this works, let's revisit "Rapunzel" from Week 1. In the four-part assignment for this week, you'll start to figure out why you like and dislike some of the characters in the story.

Part 1: Start by naming all the major characters in the story. Take a minute to come up with a list. (My list is at the end of this lesson. You can glance at it, but only after your list is finished.)

Part 2: Which of these characters do you like and which do you dislike? Put another way, which characters did you root for, which did you root against, and were there others about whom you didn't care that much either way? Before moving on, take a minute to draw three columns in your notebook: 1) Like/rooting for; 2) Dislike/rooting against; 3) Don't care. Then assign each character (from the list you created in Part 1) to one of these three columns.

After you're finished, you can glance at my columns at the end of the lesson.

Part 3: Why did you put the characters in the columns you did? Give a one-sentence answer for each one. (Once again, you can look at my answers, but only when you're finished.)

Part 4: The last part of your assignment this week is to trace even more closely how your feelings as a reader about a certain character developed as you read the story. That is, I want you to reread "Rapunzel," reprinted below, and note in the margins of the story every time you felt something new about one of the characters (which one is up to you). A very simple way to do this assignment: Every time something in the story makes you like or dislike the character you're focusing on, put the letter L (for like) or D (dislike) in the margin.

For instance, let's say I was focusing on the King's son. Note my L's and D's in the following excerpt from the story.

"After a year or two, it came to pass that the king's son rode through the forest and passed by the tower. Then he heard a song, which was so charming that he stood still and listened. It was Rapunzel, who in her solitude passed her time in letting her   L
sweet voice resound. The king's son wanted to climb up to her, and looked for the door of the tower, but none was to be found. He rode home, but the singing had so deeply touched his heart, that every day he went out into the forest and listened to it.   L

Once when he was thus standing behind a tree, he saw that an enchantress came there, and he heard how she cried: 'Rapunzel, Rapunzel, Let down your hair to me.' Then Rapunzel let down the braids of her hair, and the enchantress climbed up to her. 'If that is the ladder by which one mounts, I too will try my fortune,' said he, and the next day when it began to grow dark, he went to the tower and cried: 'Rapunzel, Rapunzel, Let down your hair to me.' Immediately the hair fell down and the king's son climbed up.   L

At first Rapunzel was terribly frightened when a man, such as her eyes had never yet beheld, came to her; but the king's son began to talk to her quite like a friend, and told her that his heart had been so stirred that it had let him have no rest, and he had been forced to see her. Then Rapunzel lost her fear, and when he asked her if she would take him for her husband, and she saw that he was young and handsome, she thought: 'He will love me more than old Dame Gothel does'; and she said yes, and laid her hand in his."   L

As you can see, I liked more than I disliked about the prince. I liked that he was charmed by Rapunzel's singing; I liked that he was resourceful enough to come up with a scheme to climb up the tower; I liked how warmly he spoke to her once he had.

Now it's your turn: Pick another character and mark up the whole story with Ls or Ds.

"Rapunzel"
by the Brothers Grimm

THERE was once a man and a woman who had long in vain wished for a child. At length the woman hoped that God was about to grant her desire. These people had a little window at the back of their house from which a splendid garden could be seen, which was full of the most beautiful flowers and herbs. It was, however, surrounded by a high wall, and no one dared to go into it because it belonged to an enchantress, who had great power and was dreaded by all the world.

One day the woman was standing by this window and looking down into the garden, when she saw a bed which was planted with the most beautiful rampion (rapunzel), and it looked so fresh and green that she longed for it, and had the greatest desire to eat some. This desire increased every day, and as she knew that she could not get any of it, she quite pined away, and looked pale and miserable. Then her husband was alarmed, and asked, "What ails you, dear wife?" "Ah," she replied, "if I can't get some of the rampion, which is in the garden behind our house, to eat, I shall die."

The man, who loved her, thought, "Sooner than let your wife die, bring her some of the rampion yourself, let it cost you what it will." In the twilight of evening, he clambered down over the wall into the garden of the enchantress, hastily clutched a handful of rampion, and took it to his wife. She at once made herself a salad of it, and ate it with much relish. She, however, liked it so much—so very much—that the next day she longed for it three times as much as before. If he was to have any rest, her husband must once more descend into the garden. In the gloom of evening, therefore, he let himself down again; but when he had clambered down the wall he was terribly afraid, for he saw the enchantress standing before him.

"How can you dare," said she with angry look, "to descend into my garden and steal my rampion like a thief? You shall suffer for it!"

"Ah," answered he, "let mercy take the place of justice, I only made up my mind to do it out of necessity. My wife saw your rampion from the window, and felt such a longing for it that she would have died if she had not got some to eat."

Then the enchantress allowed her anger to be softened, and said to him, "If the case be as you say, I will allow you to take away with you as much rampion as you will, only I make one condition. You must give me the child which your wife will bring into the world; it shall be well treated, and I will care for it like a mother." The man in his terror consented to everything, and when the woman gave birth, the enchantress appeared at once, gave the child the name of Rapunzel, and took it away with her.

Rapunzel grew into the most beautiful child beneath the sun. When she was twelve years old, the enchantress shut her into a tower, which lay in a forest, and had neither stairs nor door, but quite at the top was a little window. When the enchantress wanted to go in, she placed herself beneath this and cried,

"Rapunzel, Rapunzel, Let down your hair to me."

Rapunzel had magnificent long hair, fine as spun gold, and when she heard the voice of the enchantress she unfastened her braided tresses, wound them round one of the hooks of the window above, and then the hair fell twenty ells down, and the enchantress climbed up by it.

After a year or two, it came to pass that the King's son rode through the forest and went by the tower. Then he heard a song, which was so charming that he stood still and listened. This was Rapunzel, who in her solitude passed her time in letting her sweet voice resound. The King's son wanted to climb up to her, and looked for the door of the tower, but none was to be found. He rode home, but the singing had so deeply touched his heart, that every day he went out into the forest and listened to it. Once when he was thus standing behind a tree, he saw that an enchantress came there, and he heard how she cried,

"Rapunzel, Rapunzel, Let down your hair."

Then Rapunzel let down the braids of her hair, and the enchantress climbed up to her. "If that is the ladder by which one mounts, I will for once try my fortune," said he, and the next day when it began to grow dark, he went to the tower and cried,

"Rapunzel, Rapunzel, Let down thy hair."

Immediately the hair fell down and the King's son climbed up.

At first Rapunzel was terribly frightened when a man such as her eyes had never yet beheld, came to her; but the King's son began to talk to her quite like a friend, and told her that his heart had been so stirred that it had let him have no rest, and he had been forced to see her. Then Rapunzel lost her fear, and when he asked her if she would take him for her husband, and she saw that he was young and handsome, she thought, "He will love me more than old Dame Gothel [the enchantress] does;" and she said yes, and laid her hand in his. She said, "I will willingly go away with you, but I do not know how to get down. Bring with you a skein of silk every time that you come, and I will weave a ladder with it, and when that is ready I will descend, and you will take me on the horse."

They agreed that until that time he should come to her every evening, for the old woman came by day. The enchantress remarked nothing of this, until once Rapunzel said to her, "Tell me, Dame Gothel, how it happens that you are so much heavier for me to draw up than the young King's son—he is with me in a moment."

"Ah! you wicked child," cried the enchantress, "What do I hear you say! I thought I had separated you from all the world, and yet you have deceived me!" In her anger she clutched Rapunzel's beautiful tresses, wrapped them twice round her left hand, seized a pair of scissors with the right, and snip, snap, they were cut off, and the lovely braids lay on the ground. And she was so pitiless that she took poor Rapunzel into a desert where she had to live in great grief and misery.

On the same day, however, that she cast out Rapunzel, the enchantress in the evening fastened the braids of hair which she had cut off to the hook of the window, and when the King's son came and cried,

"Rapunzel, Rapunzel, Let down your hair," she let the hair down. The King's son ascended, but he did not find his dearest Rapunzel above, but the enchantress, who gazed at him with wicked and venomous looks. "Aha!" she cried mockingly, "You would fetch your dearest, but the beautiful bird sits no longer singing in the nest; the cat has got it, and will scratch out your eyes as well. Rapunzel is lost to you; you will never see her more."

The King's son was beside himself with pain, and in his despair he leapt down from the tower. He escaped with his life, but the thorns into which he fell pierced his eyes. Then he wandered quite blind about the forest, ate nothing but roots and berries, and did nothing but lament and weep over the loss of his dearest wife. Thus he roamed about in misery for some years, and at length came to the desert where Rapunzel lived in wretchedness. He heard a voice, and it seemed so familiar to him that he went towards it, and when he approached, Rapunzel knew him and fell on his neck and wept. Two of her tears wetted his eyes and they grew clear again, and he could see with them as before. He led her to his kingdom where he was joyfully received, and they lived for a long time afterwards, happy and contented. [4]

My answers:

My list for Part 1:

1. The husband and wife who live near the enchantress
2. The enchantress
3. Rapunzel
4. The king's son

My columns for Part 2:

Like/rooting for: Rapunzel, King's son
Dislike/rooting against: Enchantress
Don't care that much: The husband and wife who live near the enchantress

My answers for Part 3:

Rapunzel: Because she was imprisoned in a tower by the evil enchantress and banished so that she couldn't be with the prince.

King's son: Because he fell in love with Rapunzel and wandered in search of her.

Enchantress: Because she forced the man and woman who had so badly wanted a child to give it up, and because of everything she did to Rapunzel and the prince.

Husband and wife who live near the enchantress: I was prepared to like/root for these folks because their desire to have a child endeared them to me, but after the wife sent her husband into harm's way and the husband so quickly agreed to give up their child, I cooled on them. In the end, I decided that I neither liked nor disliked them.

---

4. From "Grimm's Tales" in *The Harvard Classics*, Vol. 17, ed. by Charles William Eliot (New York, 1909), pp. 71–74.

Challenge exercises:

1. Go beyond "like" and "dislike." Make more detailed notes about turning points in your feelings about characters in the story. For instance, I liked that the prince was resourceful enough to trick his way up the tower, but it was a trick all the same. On the one hand, I became a little suspicious of his cunning, on the other, impressed that he wasn't some naïve, pampered prince who had to have everything done for him.

2. Perform Part 4 of this exercise—singling out moments in the narrative that influenced your opinion of this or that character—for a story, book or film that you love.

Week 8

Who is this character? Part II

Purpose: To create a living, breathing literary character!

In the past several weeks, you've reimagined existing characters, invented characters in familiar historical situations, and taken apart stories to see how the author put characters together. It's finally time to create a character of your own, from scratch!

Let's begin by reading the opening lines of a book you may already know:

The Adventures of Robin Hood
by Howard Pyle

CHAPTER ONE

How Robin Hood Came to be an Outlaw

In merry England in the time of old, when good King Henry the Second ruled the land, there lived within the green glades of Sherwood Forest, near Nottingham Town, a famous outlaw whose name was Robin Hood. No archer ever lived that could speed a gray goose shaft with such skill and cunning as his, nor were there ever such yeomen as the sevenscore merry men that roamed with him through the greenwood shades. Right merrily they dwelled within the depths of Sherwood Forest, suffering neither care nor want, but passing the time in merry games of archery or bouts of cudgel play, living upon the King's venison, washed down with draughts of ale of October brewing.

Not only Robin himself but all the band were outlaws and dwelled apart from other men, yet they were beloved by the country people round about, for no one ever came to jolly Robin for help in time of need and went away again with an empty fist.[5]

---

5. From *The Adventures of Robin Hood*, by Howard Pyle (CreateSpace, 2010), p. 5.

Begin by looking up in the dictionary any words that are unfamiliar. (I had to look up what exactly a "glade" was, and in the way it's used here, "cudgel.")

What picture of Robin Hood and the "merry men that roamed with him" do we form from this description? Robin Hood is a crack shot; he and his merry men are a carefree bunch who lack for nothing and spend their time eating and drinking; though solitary, they command the love of the countryfolk because they help anyone who asks for it.

This week, your aim will be to write 500 words in narrative form or bullet-point form describing a character of your own.

To make things straightforward for now, let's choose a human instead of an inanimate object or animal. You may find it helpful to start by modeling the character on yourself, though remember that you have the freedom to play around with her characteristics. If you have red hair, she can have black hair. If you're tall, she can be short. If you're scared of heights, she can love jumping from roof to roof. Think back to the real-life character you changed *in part* in Week 5's exercise. In the same way, this character can have some, but not all, of your characteristics. You can also model this character on somebody you met, or somebody you've often imagined. Just make sure that you aren't copying entirely from real life.

Spend a couple of minutes thinking closely about this character. What can you say about this person that will give your audience an idea of what he or she is like? If you're stuck, answer at least 10 questions about her. You can come up with the questions yourself or answer these:

1. What's her name?

2. What does she do for fun?

3. What are her pet peeves?

4. What does she want to do when she grows up?

5. What does she want to do tomorrow?

6. If she ran away, where would she go?

7. If she could change one thing about the world, what would it be?

8. What's her favorite school subject?

9. What's her least favorite school subject?

10. If she could have a conversation with anyone, alive or dead, who would it be?

Make sure that at least 5 of these answers are different from the way you would answer for yourself.

Now, convert the portrait as it currently exists—10 answers to 10 questions—into a 500-word narrative describing this character to an audience, as Howard Pyle has done with Robin Hood and his merry men in the excerpt above.

Challenge exercise:

Very soon, we're going to move on to dialogue, and there can be no dialogue with only one character. For a challenge exercise, come up with not one but two characters. If you're stuck, think about people you've seen talking to each other over the past couple of days: A clerk to a customer; a dog owner to his dog; a football player to his coach. Any of the others in these pairs will do.

Make sure to answer the 10 questions above for each of the two characters. This information will help your dialogue in a couple of weeks.

Section 3:
Dialogue

Weeks 9–10

Week 9

Eavesdropping!

Purpose: To listen closely to the way people speak.

You can't have a short story without dialogue. Well, technically, you can, but if your stories are going to have characters, chances are they're going to have something to say. Dialogue is the word for what characters say in a story. Without it, everyone in a story would be mute.

Before we can give our characters the power of speech, we have to develop an ear for how people really talk. That might sound strange. You hear people talk all the time! But does that mean you can write good dialogue? Well, does reading many books mean you're ready to write a novel? The answer to both questions is: not yet. The reason is simple: The way we listen to other people speak is casual. The speech of others is usually background noise. We're not *really* paying attention. Even if someone is speaking directly to us, we're usually focusing on the substance of what this person is saying—clean your room; do your homework; what do you want for dinner?—than the sound of it.

That's what we're going to focus on this week: the *sound* of how people talk. You're going to be a spy. Your mission: to collect 20 snippets from 20 different conversations and jot them down in your notebook. (Try not to eavesdrop on conversations meant to be private. You can find all the dialogue you need in the conversations you have and overhear naturally throughout a day.)

Listen everywhere: at home, when the television or radio is on, at the grocery store. Listen while going on errands, or make a point of visiting a friend's house. Listen at a public place: a mall, a bowling alley, a library.

Pay attention as closely as you can: Perhaps this person swallows certain sounds? Perhaps this one drops the g's at the end of words? Maybe this one has a folksy way of speaking? Maybe this one speaks in fancy, long words? Maybe this one sounds nasal and whiny and this one speaks very quietly? Perhaps this person speaks in complete sentences, whereas this one speaks in fragments?

Also, have you ever noticed that no two voices are alike—that each person speaks with a rhythm and pronunciation and vocabulary all his own? That's what you'll be paying attention to this week.

From time to time, as you're listening, a sentence will catch your attention. It's hard to say in advance why, but something will stick with you. (If it doesn't, then just pick a sentence at random.) Write it down *immediately* and as closely to the way it was said as you can remember. Carry a pencil or pen and small notebook with you wherever you go! And listen, listen, listen. Your job is to collect 20 conversation snippets.

Challenge exercises:

1. Record 20 pairs of one-line exchanges between two people.
2. Record a single 20-line conversation between two people.

Week 10

Creating dialogue

Purpose: To craft from scratch the kind of dialogue the writer overheard last week.

This week's assignment has several parts. You'll create setting and situation, look at some examples of dialogue from classic literature, follow me through the process of creating dialogue between two of *my* characters, and then finally create your own dialogue from scratch.

Part 1: Situation and setting

This week, your character from Week 8 will come alive and speak to someone. But to whom? If you didn't do the challenge exercise, you'll have to spend some time creating a second character with whom the first can have a conversation. This requires us to briefly discuss *situation* (the occasion for these two characters to be speaking) and *setting* (the physical place where the conversation is taking place).

If the first character is someone a lot like yourself, who is the other character? Choose carefully. If you choose, say, the prime minister of Iceland, remember that these characters' conversation will somehow have to explain why an American writer is talking to the prime minister of Iceland. (Don't get me wrong—that would be unusual and fun, certainly more unusual than an everyday conversation between the first character and her mother. All I'm asking is for you to be aware of what the identity of the second character will mean for the dialogue.)

Is the first character talking to the second while standing on the ledge of a building? Sailing on a cruise? Angry about something? That's the **situation**, the *circumstances* that are bringing the characters into dialogue. The *place* where they're talking—a burning townhouse in Richmond, the Mediterranean Sea, a crowded square—is the **setting**.

So, before you can have your characters speak to each other, you'll need to think about how they came together, and where. If you're stuck, here are some ideas:

1. Let's say the first character is angry because someone in a crowded square has swiped his wallet. The character he is talking to could be a policeman. (Or a bounty hunter!)

2. The first character has entered a dance competition. If she wins, she gets a free trip to Europe to train with one of the best dancers there. You could give us a conversation between this character and another contestant, backstage, one of them having performed for the judges already, and one of them about to go on.

Both of these, you'll notice, are situations that create suspense and make us want to read on to find out what happens next.

Before you go on to Part 2, jot down ideas for situations and settings in which your characters might find themselves.

Part 2: Looking at examples of dialogue from classic literature

Before I give you an example of some dialogue written by me, how about an example from classic literature? Louisa May Alcott was a 19th-century American novelist, best known for her novel *Little Women*. Read this excerpt from her short story "Scarlet Stockings," paying special attention to what the characters say to each other and how.

"Scarlet Stockings"
by Louisa May Alcott

Chapter 1

I.
HOW THEY WALKED INTO LENNOX'S LIFE.

"COME out for a drive, Harry?"

"Too cold."

"Have a game of billiards?"

"Too tired."

"Go and call on the Fairchilds?"

"Having an unfortunate prejudice against country girls, I respectfully decline."

"What will you do then?"

"Nothing, thank you."

And settling himself more luxuriously upon the couch, Lennox closed his eyes, and appeared to slumber tranquilly. Kate shook her head, and stood regarding her brother despondently, till a sudden idea made her turn toward the window, exclaiming abruptly,

"Scarlet stockings, Harry!"

"Where?" and, as if the words were a spell to break the deepest day-dream, Lennox hurried to the window, with an unusual expression of interest in his listless face.

"I thought that would succeed! She isn't there, but I've got you up, and you are not to go down again," laughed Kate, taking possession of the sofa.

"Not a bad manoeuvre. I don't mind; it's about time for the one interesting event of the day to occur, so I'll watch for myself, thank you," and Lennox took the easy chair by the window with a shrug and a yawn.

"I'm glad any thing does interest you," said Kate, petulantly, "though I don't think it amounts to much, for, though you perch yourself at the window every day to see that girl pass, you don't care enough about it to ask her name."

"I've been waiting to be told."

"It's Belle Morgan, the Doctor's daughter, and my dearest friend."

"Then, of course, she is a blue-belle?"

"Don't try to be witty or sarcastic with her, for she will beat you at that."

"Not a dumb-belle then?"

"Quite the reverse; she talks a good deal, and very well too, when she likes."

"She is very pretty; has anybody the right to call her 'Ma belle'?"

"Many would be glad to do so, but she won't have any thing to say to them."

"A Canterbury belle in every sense of the word then?"

"She might be, for all Canterbury loves her, but she isn't fashionable, and has more friends among the poor than among the rich."

"Ah, I see, a diving-bell, who knows how to go down into a sea of troubles, and bring up the pearls worth having."

"I'll tell her that, it will please her. You are really waking up, Harry," and Kate smiled approvingly upon him.

"This page of 'Belle's Life' is rather amusing, so read away," said Lennox, glancing up the street, as if he awaited the appearance of the next edition with pleasure.

"There isn't much to tell; she is a nice, bright, energetic, warm-hearted dear; the pride of the Doctor's heart, and a favorite with every one, though she is odd."

"How odd?"

"Does and says what she likes, is very blunt and honest, has ideas and principles of her own, goes to parties in high dresses, won't dance round dances, and wears red stockings, though Mrs. Plantagenet says it's fast."

"Rather a jolly little person, I fancy. Why haven't we met her at some of the tea-fights and muffin-worries we've been to lately?"

"It may make you angry, but it will do you good, so I'll tell. She didn't care enough about seeing the distinguished stranger to come; that's the truth."

"Sensible girl, to spare herself hours of mortal dulness, gossip, and dyspepsia," was the placid reply.

"She has seen you, though, at church and dawdling about town, and she called you 'Sir Charles Coldstream' on the spot. How does that suit?" asked Kate, maliciously.

"Not bad, I rather like that. Wish she'd call some day, and stir us up."

"She won't; I asked her, but she said she was very busy, and told Jessy Tudor, she wasn't fond of peacocks."

"I don't exactly see the connection."

"Stupid boy! she meant you, of course."

"Oh, I'm peacocks, am I?"

"I don't wish to be rude, but I really do think you are vain of your good looks, elegant accomplishments, and the impression you make wherever you go. When it's worth while you exert yourself, and are altogether fascinating, but the 'I come—see—and—conquer' air you put on, spoils it all for sensible people."

"It strikes me that Miss Morgan has slightly infected you with her oddity as far as bluntness goes. Fire away, it's rather amusing to be abused when one is dying of ennui."

"That's grateful and complimentary to me, when I have devoted myself to you ever since you came. But every thing bores you, and the only sign of interest you've shown is in those absurd red hose. I should like to know what the charm is," said Kate, sharply.

"Impossible to say; accept the fact calmly as I do, and be grateful that there is one glimpse of color, life, and spirit in this aristocratic tomb of a town."

"You are not obliged to stay in it!" fiercely.

"Begging your pardon, my dove, but I am. I promised to give you my enlivening society for a month, and a Lennox keeps his word, even at the cost of his life."

"I'm sorry I asked such a sacrifice; but I innocently thought that after being away for five long years, you might care to see your orphan sister," and the dove produced her handkerchief with a plaintive sniff.

"Now, my dear creature, don't be melodramatic, I beg of you," cried her brother, imploringly. "I wished to come, I pined to embrace you, and I give you my word, I don't blame you for the stupidity of this confounded place."

"It never was so gay as since you came, for every one has tried to make it pleasant for you," cried Kate, ruffled at his indifference to the hospitable efforts of herself and friends.

"But you don't care for any of our simple amusements, because you are spoilt by the flattery, gayety, and nonsense of foreign society. If I didn't know it was half affectation, I should be in despair, you are so blase and absurd. It's always the way with men, if one happens to be handsome, accomplished, and talented, he puts on as many airs, and is as vain as any silly girl."

"Don't you think if you took breath, you'd get on faster, my dear?" asked the imperturbable gentleman, as Kate paused with a gasp.

"I know it's useless for me to talk, as you don't care a straw what I say, but it's true, and some day you'll wish you had done something worth doing all these years. I was so proud of you, so fond of you, that I can't help being disappointed, to find you with no more ambition than to kill time comfortably, no interest in any thing but your own pleasures, and only energy enough to amuse yourself with a pair of scarlet stockings."[6]

---

6. From *Scarlet Stockings*, by Louisa May Alcott (Kessinger Publishing, 2004), pp. 2–5.

Here, we have a conversation between Harry Lennox and his sister Kate. Harry is visiting for a month, and bored. Kate needles him about the only thing that makes him stir—the young woman in scarlet stockings who passes by the house every day. What did you make of the dialogue between them? It's a little more formal than the way siblings would speak to each other nowadays:

"I'm glad any thing does interest you," said Kate, petulantly, "though I don't think it amounts to much, for, though you perch yourself at the window every day to see that girl pass, you don't care enough about it to ask her name."

On the other hand, it's a nice example of the clipped way people speak in real life:

"Come out for a drive, Harry?"

"Too cold."

"Have a game of billiards?"

"Too tired."

"Go and call on the Fairchilds?"

"Having an unfortunate prejudice against country girls, I respectfully decline."

"What will you do then?"

"Nothing, thank you."

Now, look at this exchange:

"I thought that would succeed! She isn't there, but I've got you up, and you are not to go down again," laughed Kate, taking possession of the sofa.

"Not a bad manoeuvre. I don't mind; it's about time for the one interesting event of the day to occur, so I'll watch for myself, thank you," and Lennox took the easy chair by the window with a shrug and a yawn.

"I'm glad any thing does interest you," said Kate, petulantly, "though I don't think it amounts to much, for, though you perch yourself at the window every day to see that girl pass, you don't care enough about it to ask her name."

"I've been waiting to be told."

Note how the author conveys her characters' personalities. She explains a lot outright:

- "Lennox took the easy chair by the window *with a shrug and a yawn*" [my emphasis]

- "…said Kate, *petulantly*" [my emphasis]

But she also gives us hints through the dialogue:

- "I'm glad any thing does interest you" [Kate says chidingly]

- "I've been waiting to be told" [suggests Harry's laziness]

Louisa May Alcott wants us to understand that Harry is bored, spoiled, and sarcastic, while Kate is loving, girlish and fanciful. Sometimes, Alcott makes this clear in her own words; sometimes, she has her characters tell us themselves, through their dialogue.

Part 3: An example of dialogue written by me

Here's an example by me: A conversation between someone like you and a dog (except this dog can speak). This is an easy one because aren't there so many things you've always wanted to ask a dog? The dialogue between a football player and coach is likely to be more routine and predictable. (Unless, of course, a typical conversation about, say, what toppings should go on the pizzas for the team party detours into a passionate debate about the merits of pepperoni vs. sausage.)

Samantha (Don't forget to name your character.): What kind of dog are you?
Dog (You could name the dog, too.): I'm a German shepherd. What kind of human are you?
Samantha: I'm a girl. Fifth-grade. I'm nine.
Dog: I'm not too good with numbers.
Samantha: Look at your paws. How many dog fingers do you have on each paw?
Dog: Like I said…
Samantha: You have five on each paw. So if you look at all the fingers on your front left paw, that's how many grades I've been to. If you look at the fingers on both front paws, and subtract one, that's how many years I've lived.

Dog: They're not dog fingers, you know. They have a name.
Samantha: Oh. Sorry.
Dog: And each paw has four toes, not five. Actually, it depends on how you count. There's four up front, and one more in the back.
Samantha: I never knew that!
Dog: There's a lot human beings don't understand about dogs. Here's a big secret: We don't really like leashes.
Samantha: I could have guessed that.
Dog: And five years for you is like one year for us.
Samantha: I think you're better at math than you say!

It may surprise you, but I had no idea what the conversation was going to look like when I started. And even though I'm usually telling you to prepare in advance, dialogue is one department where spontaneity sometimes works better. As I've mentioned, human beings speak very differently from the way they write. When we write, we tend to be formal. When we speak, we tend to be casual. (Just think how many times you say "um" in a sentence. You rarely see "um" in a book you're reading, right?) I felt like I could catch this colloquial spontaneity by not planning too much in advance about what the characters were going to say to each other.

My starting point was simple: "What kind of dog are you?" The dog's answer was equally straightforward: "I'm a German shepherd." But then something in me decided to have the dog turn back on Samantha the same question she asked him: "What kind of human are you?" The fact that the dog asked that made me think that the dog was feeling a little talked-down-to, in general. This, in turn, started giving me ideas for the rest of the conversation. My dog was going to be slightly resentful of always being led around by humans even though he's a powerful German shepherd.

Samantha's answer consisted of three quick little sentences: "I'm a girl. Fifth grade. I'm nine." Here, I was trying to catch the way Samantha might speak in real life, as I explained above. As you might recall from the eavesdropping exercise, people don't speak in complete, well-turned sentences. They break sentences off in the middle, speak in fragments. I think Samantha's dialogue here *sounds* a lot more believable, than "I'm a girl who attends the fifth grade at such-and-such school." Just say that sentence out loud. Does anybody speak this way?

Now, I didn't know where the dialogue should go next, but I decided, higher up, that my dog was going to be a little ornery. So he was probably going to say something not unfriendly, but not too friendly, either. What could he respond to in what Samantha said? That's when I thought: Hey, do dogs even understand numbers? (The answer could have been anything. When we write fiction, our dogs can be mute or rocket scientists. That's the beauty of creative writing. Anything is possible. We just have to justify it by developing it in credible detail.)

I hope this gives you an idea of how I created the dialogue: I "listened" to what the characters were saying and mixed in a little bit of my own made-up troublemaking to stir the pot.

Part 4: Write your own dialogue

When your characters speak, you may be surprised by the things they start saying. This is called "listening to the character." You've given your characters names, traits, likes and dislikes; now, your clay sculptures are ready to come to life. And when they do, they often take on a life of their own, the same way kids do, surprising their parents. So don't be afraid to "listen" to your characters. You might have planned to have them have a conversation about homework, but a passing remark by one of them about the downed tree she saw on the way to school might set them off on a tangent about chainsaws and beavers (in other words, ways of cutting through a downed tree). Don't be afraid to follow this tangent. Don't force your characters to talk about what *you* want them to talk about. Let them say what *they* want to say, if that makes sense.

It's your turn to write some dialogue. Fill two pages, single-spaced, in your notebook—about 500 words—with dialogue between the characters you've created, in the situation and setting you've decided on. As in the above example of Samantha speaking to the dog, every time a different character speaks, that should begin a new line in your notebook.

Challenge exercise:

Go online to a website like simplyscripts.com or imsdb.com (Internet Movie Script Database) and find the script for a movie you've never seen, ideally based on a short story or a book. Read the script, trying to imagine what a movie based on it would look like. Then watch the movie. Did the movie look anything like what you imagined from the script?

Notice the enormous difference between following a story on film and on the page. Movies can add many visual cues to the dialogue to help you understand what's going on. As a result, the dialogue in a film can be a lot more "spare;" that is, undetailed. In fiction, the writer has to provide that clarifying information using words, relying on quite a bit of dialogue or description to convey the same thing as a second-long facial expression by an actor on screen. (This is what explains the clichéd expression "A picture is worth a thousand words." More on clichés in the poetry section.)

Last, read the short story or book on which the film was based, reflecting on how differently dialogue works in the two.

Section 4:
Observation

Weeks 11–12

Week 11

Who am I?

Purpose: To learn how to observe an object closely.

Have you ever thought about something *a lot*, or paid attention to something very closely? For instance, have you ever, upon seeing a bug on a leaf, gotten *really* close to examine the bug for as long as it lets you, taking in every little detail of its coat and wings and eyes and legs? Have you noticed that bugs really like to rub their front legs together as if they're really excited about a delicious meal they're about to sit down to? Or that snow that has turned to ice will trap inside itself all sorts of curious things? After this exercise, you might.

This week, you're going to observe something very closely. Take the table at which you're sitting. Can you say 10 specific things about it? (Or, for something a little more interesting, how about your dream car, or anything at all that you've dreamt about, like a drum set, or a new outfit?)

Here are 10 questions you can use to help you come up with 10 specific observations about the table. (If you decide to describe something else, you may have to adjust the questions below to make them fit.)

1. What color is it?
2. What shape is it?
3. How many chairs does it fit?
4. Is it smooth on the surface?
5. Of what kind of wood is it made?
6. Is there anything on the desk, like placemats or a pen holder?
7. Are the legs straight or curved?
8. Does it fold out?
9. Does it have any marks?
10. What is its size (length, width, height)?

As you can see, you can notice a lot about even a simple old table. Now that you've had some practice, here's your exercise for the week.

Part 1: Your job in the first part of this exercise is to pick an object and provide 10 descriptions of it, such as "has long legs" or "is brown with polka dots," to your mentor, who will have to guess what it is. Don't worry too much about giving away the object; focus on coming up with 10 characteristics.

If you're stuck, you might get some help by responding to the Five Senses. You know what they ask:

• How does it taste?
• What does it smell like?
• How does it feel?
• What does it sound like?
• What does it look like?

If you can answer these five questions, you'll be well on your way to describing the object.

Keep in mind the different characteristics you're likely to come up with for specific and general objects. If you decide to describe "snow," you'll have to say general things like "I am white" and "You see me in the winter." But if you decide to describe a very specific ball of snow (with a carrot for a nose and black buttons for eyes, say) outside your house right now, you could say things like "You walk by me to get inside our house."

Part 2: Before you show your group of 10 to your mentor, see if you can organize it from the most general ("You see me in the winter") to the most specific ("I have a carrot for a nose"). A handy rule to distinguish **general** from **specific** is that general characteristics could apply to the item you're thinking of as well as to many others, whereas specific characteristics probably refer only to the thing you're thinking of (and will probably tip off your guesser right away). In fact, when you make your list, make sure that #10—your most specific description—couldn't describe anything else.

Here's one that I did. Can you guess what I am?

1. I am a rectangle.
2. I am numbered.
3. I have glue in my spine.

4. Once, I was a tree.

5. Without electricity, you can't use me at night.

6. That's okay, because you use me most often in the morning.

7. Sometimes, I'm funny. Sometimes, I'm educational. Sometimes, I'm just a chore.

8. I am open, except when I'm closed.

9. You write inside me.

10. There are 36 items in my belly.

Put your best guess down here: _____

(The answer is at the bottom of this page.)

Notice how the characteristics proceed from general ("I am a rectangle"—that could refer to a notebook, a refrigerator, or a house) to specific ("There are 36 items in my belly.")

Your turn. Write down 10 characteristics and ask your mentor to guess.

1. _____

2. _____

3. _____

4. _____

5. _____

6. _____

7. _____

8. _____

9. _____

10. _____

Challenge exercises:

1. Convert your 10-point description into 250 words of narrative.

2. Write a 250-word description of an action, like a ballerina dancing.

Answer: I am this book!

Week 12

The scene

Purpose: To observe a scene very closely.

Last week, you applied your fiction writer's microscope to an object. This week you're going to do the same thing for a moving target: A scene. You can make notes about what's going on in the scene in narrative form or as bullet points. Make sure to write for at least 500 words.

Now, what would qualify as a scene worth observing? Just like last week, you don't have to look far. Perhaps your father is mowing the lawn. You might describe it this way:

"Dad is outside, mowing the lawn in his old, red-and-blue hockey jersey. The mower revs and buzzes like a razor in a barbershop. The blades of grass stick to his bare shins, the jersey, his forehead. He wipes his forehead with a sleeve and takes a long, satisfied swig from the pitcher of lemonade my sister and I brought out to him earlier. The heat is so thick, you can practically feel it through the window."

And so on. Notice that I relied on the Five Senses for help: I described the *sound* of the lawnmower, the *feeling* of the heat through the window, the *sight* of Dad working, etc. Other than that, I simply described what was in front of me, including the things it made me think of ("like a razor in a barbershop"). If I wanted to go off on a tangent about the last time I was in a barbershop, or the last time Dad cut my hair, that would be fine.

Here are some other ideas for scenes to observe:

Go to a public place, like the mall, the library, or a restaurant. At the mall, wander into a store. At the library, hang out by the lending desk. At a restaurant, can you see anything noteworthy going on in the kitchen, or among the waiters? My point is that you don't have to seek out anything especially eventful to write a compelling description of a scene. There are surprisingly interesting and noteworthy things going on even in the most mundane situations, as long as we pay close enough attention to them. However, if something eventful *is* going on in your town or home—a concert, a visit from family friends—feel free to focus on that. But if you're describing, say, that visit from family friends, choose a specific moment to focus on, such as dinner one night. Otherwise, you'll find yourself having filled 500 words very quickly. Remember: The point of this exercise isn't to write a diary entry describing everything that happened during the weekend your cousins visited. It's to describe one limited moment/scene very, very closely, such as 5–10 minutes of Dad mowing the lawn.

Challenge exercise:

You've observed an object and a scene. Now describe a person's physical appearance with the same level of detail. Same rules apply: 500 words in narrative or bullet-point form.

Section 5:
Setting

Weeks 13–14

Week 13

Describing place

Purpose: To observe a place closely.

In the last section, you described an object and a scene with microscopic closeness. This week, as we move into a section on setting, you will do the same thing for a place. *Setting*, you'll remember, refers to where a story takes place. Before I ask you to try your hand at a description of your own, let's look at a published example of what I mean. Read the beginning of "Rip Van Winkle," a short story by the great 19th century American writer Washington Irving, below. Note the close description of the Catskill Mountains in the first paragraph and the village and cottage in the second.

Rip Van Winkle
by Washington Irving

Whoever has made a voyage up the Hudson must remember the Kaatskill mountains. They are a dismembered branch of the great Appalachian family, and are seen away to the west of the river, swelling up to a noble height, and lording it over the surrounding country. Every change of season, every change of weather, indeed, every hour of the day, produces some change in the magical hues and shapes of these mountains, and they are regarded by all the good wives, far and near, as perfect barometers. When the weather is fair and settled, they are clothed in blue and purple, and print their bold outlines on the clear evening sky; but, sometimes, when the rest of the landscape is cloudless, they will gather a hood of gray vapors about their summits, which, in the last rays of the setting sun, will glow and light up like a crown of glory.

At the foot of these fairy mountains, the voyager may have descried the light smoke curling up from a village, whose shingle-roofs gleam among the trees, just where the blue tints of the upland melt away into the fresh green of the nearer landscape. It is a little village, of great antiquity, having been founded by some of the Dutch colonists in the early times of the province, just about the beginning of the government of the good Peter Stuyvesant, (may he rest in peace!) and there were some of the houses of the original settlers standing within a few years, built of small yellow bricks brought from Holland, having latticed windows and gable fronts, surmounted with weathercocks.[7]

---

7. From *Rip Van Winkle and The Legend of Sleepy Hollow,* by Washington Irving (New York, 1893), pp. 19–20.

Washington Irving must have paid very close attention to the mountains and the cottages to describe them in such detail.

This week, you will describe a place for 500 words in narrative form, just as Washington Irving did. As in preceding lessons, you don't need to look very far to find a suitable place. Observe your yard: a lot more happens there than you think. Describe the shape of the trees, the outline of the landscape, whether there are any objects crowding the grass. If there is a woods nearby, take a walk and describe what they look like. If there is an interesting building in town, describe that. Or, you can zoom out and describe the town itself. (You'll have to be judicious in choosing what to describe, as you can go on for quite a while describing something as big as the town in which you live.)

When you describe place, you don't have to limit yourself to physical characteristics, as Washington Irving mostly did. You can deploy the Five Senses. You can also share interesting historical details or tell stories. And if a physical characteristic, like a war memorial, reminds you of something, like the fact that a friend's brother served in the Army, you can detour to discuss that. A place is more than the collection of its physical characteristics. It's also the sum of its residents and their stories.

Challenge exercises:

1. Write 500 words imagining what the place looked like 500 years ago.

2. Write 500 words imagining what the place will look like 500 years from now.

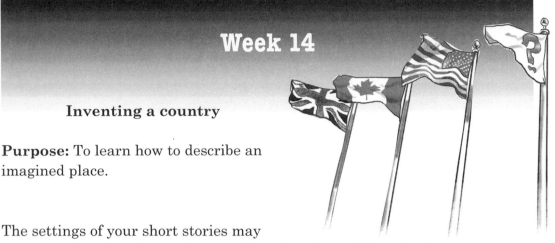

Week 14

Inventing a country

Purpose: To learn how to describe an imagined place.

The settings of your short stories may draw on places you know. Just as often, though, you'll need to invent your settings, either because the settings are completely imaginary or because you want to change key details about real places.

This week, you'll practice inventing setting from scratch.

Part 1:

Take a piece of paper and your favorite drawing implement—pencil, pen, paint. Even if you don't like to draw, give this a try. The result doesn't have to be professional. Some squiggles will do just fine. Now, draw a symbol. A symbol is something that stands for something else, like a code or shorthand. This symbol must represent a mythical country from which you are a representative to the country in which you live, be it the United States, the United Kingdom, Canada, Australia, or New Zealand.

You have to tell us 1) what the symbol is called (in the invented language of your country) and 2) what it tells us about the country from which you come. For instance, if your symbol is a tree, it could symbolize the fact that in your country, everyone is required by law to care for nature and the environment. Or it could mean that every person, when she turns 18, receives a tree from the government, which she plants and which grows alongside her. This is a **literal** possibility; that is, the tree stands for a tree, or nature. But your symbol could also be **abstract**; that is, it may not be understandable to anyone but yourself, or its definition may not make obvious sense. You could draw a top hat and say that it stands for sports, which every citizen in your nation is required to play. Or you could draw a field of squiggly lines and say *that* stands for sports. It's really up to you.

Your symbol needs a name in the language of the country from which you come. It could be a completely invented sound like micapula (mee-ka-poo-la), and it could mean "the tree" or "honoring and respecting the Earth and its four elements is the law in our nation." The details are up to you.

So, to recap, your job is to:

1. Draw a symbol

2. Give it a name in your country's language

3. Tell us what the name stands for

Part 2:

Now tell us a bit more about your country. What is it called? Who's in charge? Remember, the information doesn't have to resemble what's true for the country in which you live. The leader of your country doesn't have to be a man, or even a human being. And your country doesn't have to have one leader; it could have another system of governance. Which one exactly is up to you. It could be a "real" country or not; it can be modeled on a "real" country or not. (As in Week 5's character exercise, you may find it helpful to start from a location you know, and then alter some of the details.) Either tell us 10 things in list form (at least one sentence each) or write 500 words of description in narrative form.

If you're stuck, answer these 10 questions:

1. What do your citizens like to eat?

2. Is your country friendly to the United States, or to the United Kingdom, or to Canada? To the nation of Ugadougou? Why or why not?

3. What is the geography of your country? Is it flat or hilly? Does it have a coastline? If so, what body of water does it border?

4. When did your country come into existence? How did that happen?

5. What kind of rules does it have? Is recycling mandatory? Are people free to drive on both sides of the road?

6. Speaking of which, how do people get around? Foot, bicycle, monkey?

7. What was the most popular book in your country last year? (Do your citizens read? Or do they have other forms of entertainment, like seeing who can outrace a cloud moving over a field?)

8. Does your country go to the Olympics? In what sports does it excel?

9. What is the size of your country and where is it located? Is it on Planet Earth?

10. If you could change one thing about your country, what would it be?

Challenge exercises:

1. Draw a map of the country your symbol represents. The country could take any shape, but you should divide it into regions. The names of the regions are up to you. Make sure to mark the capital, as well.

2. Pick one of the regions and tell us about its climate, how many people live there, what the people there like to eat, what the region produces (coffee, bananas, fish, what kind of fish?), and how long it takes to get from there to the capital.

Section 6:
Point of View

Weeks 15–17

Week 15

Point of view

Purpose: To learn the difference between first-person and third-person narration.

Compare the beginnings of two stories:

The Boscombe Valley Mystery
by Sir Arthur Conan Doyle

We were seated at breakfast one morning, my wife and I, when the maid brought in a telegram. It was from Sherlock Holmes and ran in this way:

Have you a couple of days to spare? Have just been wired for from the west of England in connection with Boscombe Valley tragedy. Shall be glad if you will come with me. Air and scenery perfect. Leave Paddington by the 11:15.

"What do you say, dear?" said my wife, looking across at me. "Will you go?"

"I really don't know what to say. I have a fairly long list at present."

"Oh, Anstruther would do your work for you. You have been looking a little pale lately. I think that the change would do you good, and you are always so interested in Mr. Sherlock Holmes's cases."

"I should be ungrateful if I were not, seeing what I gained through one of them," I answered. "But if I am to go, I must pack at once, for I have only half an hour." My experience of camp life in Afghanistan had at least had the effect of making me a prompt and ready traveller. My wants were few and simple, so that in less than the time stated I was in a cab with my valise, rattling away to Paddington Station.[8]

The Bride Comes to Yellow Sky
by Stephen Crane

The great pullman was whirling onward with such dignity of motion that a glance from the window seemed simply to prove that the plains of Texas were pouring eastward. Vast flats of green grass, dull-hued spaces of mesquite and cactus, little groups of frame houses, woods of light and tender trees, all were sweeping into the east, sweeping over the horizon, a precipice.

---

8. From *Adventures of Sherlock Holmes* by Sir Arthur Conan Doyle (New York, 1892), p. 76.

A newly married pair had boarded this coach at San Antonio. The man's face was reddened from many days in the wind and sun, and a direct result of his new black clothes was that his brick-colored hands were constantly performing in a most conscious fashion. From time to time he looked down respectfully at his attire. He sat with a hand on each knee, like a man waiting in a barber's shop. The glances he devoted to other passengers were furtive and shy.

The bride was not pretty, nor was she very young. She wore a dress of blue cashmere, with small reservations of velvet here and there and with steel buttons abounding. She continually twisted her head to regard her puff sleeves, very stiff, straight, and high. They embarrassed her. It was quite apparent that she had cooked, and that she expected to cook, dutifully. The blushes caused by the careless scrutiny of some passengers as she had entered the car were strange to see upon this plain, under-class countenance, which was drawn in placid, almost emotionless lines. [9]

What's one of the big differences between these excerpts? They're being told from different points of view. An "I" character is telling the first story. In the second example, some unknown "third-person" narrator is.

We all know what point of view is. In ordinary speech, it means something close to "opinion," as in "What's your point of view on the situation in the Middle East?" In short stories, "point of view" means something closer to "Who's telling the story?"

There are many possible points of view, but in storytelling, two are the most common. The first is called **first-person** point of view. That's when a story is told from the point of view of an "I." (Example: "I was an old man when the birds came to town.") The second is called **third-person**: That's when the narrator refers to all the characters as "he," "she," or "they." So, like Stephen Crane's "The Bride Comes to Yellow Sky," whose opening is above, "Rapunzel" and Louisa May Alcott's "The Scarlet Stockings" both have third-person narrators. If Rapunzel decided to tell her story from her own point of view, the fairy tale would become first-person.

Let's practice first-person vs. third-person narration. Take your write-up about the historical character you invented in Week 6. Did you write it in first- or third-person?

---

9. From *The Best Short Stories of Stephen Crane by Stephen Crane* (Digireads.com, 2008), pp. 38–39.

Your assignment this week is simple: Rewrite it from the other point of view. Same length: 500 words. As you make the changes, think about the ways in which the story reads differently from this new point of view.

Challenge exercises:

1. Take the opening lines of "Robin Hood" from Week 8 and rewrite them in the first person from the perspective of Robin Hood. (Same number of words.)

2. Preview of next week's lesson on motive: Rewrite the opening lines of "Robin Hood" from the perspective of the Sheriff of Nottingham, whose job is to catch and imprison "outlaws" like Robin Hood. Think about how differently the Sheriff would see the characteristics described by the narrator.

Week 16

Point of view (motive)

Purpose: To think about how a story changes depending on the interests of whoever is telling it.

Last week, we talked about different points of view in narration: first-person (an "I" telling the story) vs. third-person (a narrator who isn't one of the characters). Regardless of who's telling the story, it's important to remember that the narrator has his own motives and interests, and that if another character got to tell the story, she would probably put a different spin on things. This week, we're going to acquaint ourselves with how a story might change depending on the perspective of who's telling it.

You're going to pick a **situation** out of the options that follow and give us the **dialogue** of both sides as they present their versions of the story. Imagine yourself as a lawyer who is arguing both sides in a case. Write at least 500 words of dialogue, where each new line of dialogue begins a new line in your notebook.

1. There's been a car accident and a police officer is trying to understand what happened. Driver A is claiming one thing and Driver B another. What are they saying?

2. Mom is very upset because a flowerbed in the yard has been trampled. John says it was the dog. Sylvia says it was John (they're siblings). Tell us what each is claiming happened. (Mom can speak, too.)

3. Rebecca thinks that it's Sam's turn to clean the house; Sam thinks it's Rebecca's. Tell us why each of them thinks so.

Challenge exercises:

1. Come up with a scenario of your own where the two characters are likely to argue something very different from each other. Write their dialogue as per the instructions in the lesson.

2. Convert your dialogue, either from this week's assignment or from the challenge exercise, above, into two 500-word statements from each of the characters. These don't have to read like fiction. Imagine they're statements the characters are submitting to a jury that will have to decide who is right.

3. Write 500 words on a topic from your own point of view, and another 500 from the point of view of someone who disagrees with you. Alternative: Name something about which your opinions have changed, such as a friend, a toy, or a hobby. Write 500 words as a person who loves that thing and another 500 as someone who no longer does.

Week 17

Point of view (mood)

Purpose: To learn how a story changes depending on the mood of the narrator.

This exercise is a modified version of a famous exercise created by John Gardner, who was a novelist and greatly respected teacher of fiction who died at the very young age of 49 in a motorcycle accident. (Forty-nine may not seem like a young age to you now, but trust me—it is.) This week, you're going to describe a barn. That's right, a simple old barn. You're free to imagine whatever you want: the cows near the barn, the color of the paint, the smell inside, the feel of the boards, anything at all. (Remember the Five Senses!)

Here's the thing, though: Your assignment is to describe the barn not once, but twice. The first time, you're going to describe the barn as someone who's really happy. In the second example, you're going to describe the same barn as someone who's really sad. Don't tell us that the first character is happy or that the second character is sad, though you may wish to figure out for yourself why they are. In fact, it's probably a very good idea to come up with some explanation to yourself.

I hope you'll agree that these two people are likely to see the same things very differently. In fact, they're liable to notice completely different things! One might notice the barn's new paint job; the other might see it as an ugly job using the wrong color. One might notice the contented-seeming cows, the other the singed grass. But things don't have to work predictably in this way, where the happy person sees the glass half full and the sad person is a pessimist. The happy person might see a barn in complete ruin, but he may be teeming with new plans for it; he could rhapsodize about all the wonderful things that he's going to improve about his barn! And in the case of the sad person, he might be looking at a state-of-the-art barn—there might even be a robot who milks the cows!—but can find no joy in it because he's so depressed.

Whenever you're describing something that isn't in front of you and you're stuck, use the Five Senses:

How does it taste?

What does it smell like?

How does it feel?

What does it sound like?

What does it look like?

For each viewpoint, write 500 words. These should be more than notes for a story or casual observations. You should compose these words *as if they are part of an actual short story*. You, the author, are giving us 500 words on a character's view of this barn. You can present that view in first-person or third-person. If you need an example, refer back to the "Rip Van Winkle" opener that begins Week 13's lesson. While it isn't explicitly concerned with shifting points of view, it's an excellent example of the kind of description I have in mind.

Challenge exercises:

1. Go beyond description to explore other means of storytelling. Pick either the happy or sad scenario, and write *it* in two different ways. For instance, 500 words of, say, the barn's new owner discussing it with a spouse or a hired hand. ("I don't know, Tom. It's new, but it looks like a science lab. I wanted a farm.") The other 500 words can be an internal monologue, in which the new barn owner thinks about it out loud or in his mind: "John Till glanced around the warped boards and sighed. It didn't look all that bad in the catalogue but now I don't know..., he thought...".

2. Forget the barn. Write 500 "happy" words and 500 "sad" words about a character's perception of... whatever you'd like.

Section 7:
Write a Short Story from Scratch

Week 18

Week 18

Write a short story from scratch

Purpose: To write a short story from scratch.

You've been working toward it all course long, and the time has come: This week, you're going to write a short story from scratch. The plot will be up to you; so will the characters, the dialogue, the setting—just about everything. This week, aim for a story at least 1000 words long. This may seem like a lot, but it's only twice as long as many of your assignments. And remember that those were assignments highlighting one aspect of a story. Your actual story will include lots of different aspects, so you will reach that limit before you know it.

How should you approach the writing of a story from scratch? You may want to revisit one of the early lessons on coming up with story ideas. Once you've got one, work your way through the course to refresh your memory on the building blocks of a story. Who are your characters? What do they want? What stands in their way? What do they look like? What are they going to talk about? Where is all of this taking place? Before launching into your story, you may wish to practice by composing a paragraph about the appearance of one of your characters, or a description of a scene involving two characters, or a physical description of an object or place, such as what you encountered in Washington Irving's "Rip Van Winkle."

When you're ready, tell the story. Remember that in writing it, you won't be telling it very differently than you would if you were telling it to someone verbally. The bones of the story will be the same: This happened, then that happened. The big difference is that you are going to tell it with a little bit more attention to the nuances of storytelling—character, dialogue, setting, imagination, etc.—than someone casually telling someone else about "this crazy thing that happened."

Have fun! You've earned it.

Mentor Materials

for

Part I: FICTION

Mentor Materials

Section 1: Plot
Weeks 1–4

Week 1—Plot points
Purpose: To understand how stories come together.

Here's what a sample list of plot points from "Rapunzel" might look like:

1. An enchantress catches a man stealing rampion from her garden and lets him go in exchange for his first-born.
2. The enchantress locks up the little girl, named Rapunzel, in a high tower without stairs or a door.
3. The enchantress visits Rapunzel by climbing up her long hair.
4. One day, the King's son happens upon Rapunzel's sweet song, but can't climb up to her until he overhears the enchantress instructing Rapunzel to let down her hair.
5. The King's son does the same thing. In the tower, he and Rapunzel declare their love for each other.
6. Rapunzel tells the King's son to bring silk so she can weave a ladder to escape.
7. One day, Rapunzel accidentally reveals the plan to the enchantress.
8. The enchantress cuts Rapunzel's hair, banishes her to a desert, and tricks the King's son into climbing up to the tower by lowering Rapunzel's hair.
9. Cursed by the enchantress and heartbroken by Rapunzel's banishment, the prince leaps out of the tower, and his eyes are pierced by thorns.
10. He wanders until he discovers Rapunzel, whose tears return his eyesight, and they live happily ever after.

It might help to not limit the writer to 10 points in the first draft of the outline. Let her create as many plot points as she wishes. Then, in the second draft of the summary, she can focus on combining and cutting.

It's not the end of the world if the writer ends up with more than 10. It's an arbitrary number for the purposes of this exercise. The aim of this lesson isn't so much to learn how to outline as to see how plot points lead to a story. For instance, in my first draft of the outline, I devoted the first two plot points to the couple that had long been dreaming of a child. I cut them out in the second draft because, as important as they are, they vanish after the opening lines, and there's so much else of import that happens in the story.

If the writer is stuck, prompt her with questions:

1. Is the enchantress Rapunzel's mother? If not, how does Rapunzel become her ward?
2. How does the King's son learn of Rapunzel?
3. How does the enchantress trick the prince into climbing up to the tower after she's banished Rapunzel?
4. What happens when the prince gets up there?
5. Does the prince find his way back to Rapunzel?
6. Will the story outline still make sense if we cut out mention of the husband and wife who gave birth to Rapunzel? If we cut out Rapunzel?

Week 2—Come up with 10 story ideas
Purpose: To practice coming up with the essential building block of a story: the story idea.

Remind the writer that, in coming up with a story idea, "unusual" doesn't have to mean "extraordinary." Beginning writers often overreach, imagining that a story must have aliens invading Earth to count as a story. (Just as often, they underreach, imagining that nothing more unusual and suspenseful than the regular day they just had is necessary.)

If the writer is stuck, ask him to pick an object—any object, even something prosaic. Then ask him to describe the usual purpose of this object. Then ask how something unusual could befall this object. You'll be surprised by how even the most mundane objects harbor potential as focal points for stories. Even that toaster becomes interesting when it suddenly stops requiring electricity to do its work.

The two keywords for coming up with story ideas at this stage are: "suspense" and "unusual." Questions to ask the writer: Will this make you/the reader want to find out what happens next?

You may also choose to have the writer do the challenge exercise *before* embarking on the lesson's assignment as a way of becoming comfortable with story ideas. For more story ideas toward which you can nudge the writer, look at Week 4, where I mention some others.

Week 3—Turn a photograph into a story
Purpose: To come up with a plot using the image in a photograph.

To practice, you might choose a famous image like the Times Square Kiss or the raising of the American flag over Iwo Jima. The latter, especially, presents an opportunity for the writer to investigate some history alongside this week's lesson. The Iwo Jima image is useful as well because while its history may not be known yet to the writer, its meaning is fairly easy to decipher: Soldiers are raising an American flag.

Why are they raising an American flag, you might ask. Because they won a battle, the writer might respond. A battle against whom? Here, the writer, if she doesn't know about the war against Japan, might say something incorrect but imaginative like: "Aliens." Go with this direction: Did the aliens attack the U.S.? What happened? Tease a narrative out of the writer, step-by-step, by asking questions based on her answers in this way.

In any lesson, you can help yourself come up with questions to prompt the writer by brainstorming around what might be called the **5 Essential Ingredients of Fiction**: plot, characters, dialogue, setting, point of view. Go through each of these categories, applying them to the image/story idea/etc. at hand:

- What's happening here? (plot)
- Who are the characters? (character)
- What are they saying to each other? (dialogue)
- Where is this taking place? (setting)
- Who's telling the story? (point of view)

For this week specifically, here's a list of sample questions that could apply to any image:

- What do we see in the image?
- What's the setting? Are we indoors or outdoors? If outdoors, what's the weather? If indoors, where are we? A department store, a baseball

diamond, a homeless shelter, a battlefield?
- Who are the characters, if any?
- Do they know each other? What do they think of each other?
- What can we tell about them, based on their mood or the way they are dressed?
- If we could ask them "What do you want?", what would they say?
- Let's imagine where these characters were at this time yesterday.
- Let's imagine what this place looked like on another occasion.
- Why are the characters doing what they're doing?

Week 4—Map out a story idea with plot points

Purpose: To take a story idea one step closer to a finished story by plotting out, step-by-step, what will happen in the story.

If the writer is stuck for ideas about what happens next, or how to begin, prompt him with questions. If the story idea is "Mom comes home from the grocery store acting weird," you might say "Weird how?" or "What does Mom usually do when she gets home from the grocery store?" The writer might say, "She puts the groceries away." Then you might say, "So, wouldn't it strike you as strange if she did something different from that? What might that be? Would it be weird if she sat down and started eating cereal directly from the box without having put anything away?" When the writer answers affirmatively, you might ask: "What would you do if you saw that? Might you not ask Mom why she was doing that, or if she was hungry? And wouldn't it be strange if Mom said no, she wasn't hungry at all, then rose to put the groceries away?" And so on.

As discussed last week, you might lean on the 5 Essential Ingredients of Fiction. Let's say the story idea is "Mr. Smith's car runs out of gas on a deserted highway at night."

Potential questions:

Plot: What happened? Did Mr. Smith forget to fill up? Or is there a leak in his tank? If there's a leak, is that because the car is faulty or someone punctured his tank? If the car is faulty, is it a rental or his own car? If his own, is Mr. Smith not very vigilant or skilled at taking care of automobiles?

Notice that, inevitably, plot overlaps with character: Asking what happened leads to us to wonder whether it happened because the character is not vigilant or skilled at taking care of vehicles. The 5 Essential Ingredients of Fiction is just a brainstorming tool: It's meant to get you thinking about essential aspects of the story. Your questions will ultimately overlap categories.

Generally, you can imagine your questions to the writer as a kind of choose-your-own-adventure. If the writer says the car is a rental, for instance, you might ask: Did he rent it at the airport? Where did he fly in from, and why? (Touches on setting.) If Mr. Smith owns the car, you might ask something else, like whether he isn't very good at taking care of vehicles.

Proceed down the list of the 5 Essentials:

- **Dialogue**: Does Mr. Smith have a cell phone? Is it getting a signal in this emptiness? Did he call his wife earlier? Speaking of which, is he married? Does anyone know where he is? If he can get a signal, can he call police?

- **Setting**: Where is he going, anyway? Why is he out so late at night in such an empty place? Was he rushing somewhere? What season is it? If it's winter, is he in danger of freezing to death?

- **Point of view**: Is Mr. Smith telling us the story? Is he telling it to us as it's happening or after the fact? If after the fact, that must mean he didn't die there in the cold night, right?

There are other categories you might include in your repertoire, such as:

- **Description**: What kind of car is it? What is Mr. Smith wearing, and what does it tell us about his background? (Touches on character.) And so on.

Mentor Materials

Section 2: Character
Weeks 5–8

Week 5—Who is this character?

Purpose: To invent situations for real-life characters and imagine their behavior based on what you already know about them.

Character and plot are closely linked. There are many teachers of writing who say that "character *is* plot," meaning that nothing other than what occurs to a character should constitute the plot of a story. Even if that's too extreme, knowing how to draw believable, compelling characters is one of the central challenges of creative writing. Think about Madame Bovary, Ignatius J. Reilly from *A Confederacy of Dunces*, Hamlet. The things that happen to these characters are more or less ordinary. Hamlet's situation is perhaps more extraordinary than Ignatius J. Reilly's, but ultimately, we read on not only to find out what happens, but because we'll follow these characters anywhere. Their struggles have been made fascinating to us by authors who have brought them to life as credibly and nuanced as if they were flesh-and-blood human beings.

This week, you'll be helping the writer take her first steps toward creating an equally unforgettable character. The lesson explores character using real-life characters whom the writer can use as a springboard to imagination. If the writer is stuck in either part of the exercise, help by prompting with questions. Where have you seen this person? What were they wearing? Are they friendly? The situations in which the writer has observed the character will lead you to questions that will tease out more information. (Remember the 5 Essentials!) The substance of those answers will, in turn, suggest a fictional situation in which the writer can observe her half-real, half-fictional character.

For more questions that you might use as prompts, look ahead to Week 6.

Week 6—Historical characters

Purpose: To imagine new details about characters who really existed.

If necessary, you can use any of the following questions to jump-start the writer's imagination.

• What country are you from? What is your name?
• How old are you?
• What family do you have? (Wife, children, parents, siblings?) Which family members are still alive? What happened to the others?
• What is your favorite food? Your favorite pastime?
• What do you look like?
• How did you find out about/get involved in the event?
• What do you like best about your current situation/life? What do you hate about it?
• What do you hope your future will look like?
• What countries have you visited?
• Are you wealthy or poor?
• Are you good at what you do? Do you like your work, or have you been forced to do it against your will?
• Who is your best friend?
• Who are your coworkers? Do you like them? Which one is your favorite?
• Which one do you like the least?
• What is your greatest dream in life?
• What has your biggest disappointment been?
• Have you ever broken a bone, been seriously ill, been afraid for your life? If so, when?

Week 7—Heroes and villans

Purpose: To figure out why we like some characters and dislike others.

This exercise resembles Week 1 in that it "dismantles" characters to show the writer how they might be built from scratch. Our feelings about the enchantress are a cumulative response to prompts by the authors. When the writer writes her own story, she'll have to work with the same kinds of prompts. The best way to get a reader to like a character is to have the character do something nice, or to have something mean done to the character. The opposite is just as true. This is obviously a very simplistic shorthand, but it's a good starting point for a beginner.

Help the writer by moving with her through the story and asking how each new revelation about the character's personality makes her feel. Do we like the enchantress for locking up Rapunzel? Why or why not? Do we like the king's son for climbing up to see Rapunzel every night? Why or why not? Do we like Rapunzel for living in wretchedness in the desert? Why or why not? The idea here is to get the writer to become conscious of how the characters act—and how the Brothers Grimm shaped our notions of these characters through those actions.

Week 8—Who is this character?: Part II

Purpose: To create a living, breathing literary character!

We started this section by working with existing characters and then moved on to the more advanced task of creating them from scratch. That it's easier to tweak something that already exists than create something from whole cloth is only part of the reason. The other is that fiction is profoundly autobiographical, even when that isn't literally the case. Writers endow their characters with their own (real or wished-for) characteristics, and with observations they themselves have had; they create plots that reflect subjects of concern to them.

So, in creating a brand-new character, it may help to start by asking the writer to say 10 things about himself. You can use the following categories:

Physical appearance: Long hair or short? Color of eyes? Other distinguishing features?

Dress: Jeans and t-shirt or dress?

Personality: Irritable, patient, bright, hard-working, lazy?

Pet peeves: Hates losing a sock in the laundry? Doing laundry? Siblings who don't put their dishes in the sink?

Favorite things in the world: Mint chocolate chip ice cream? A freshly mown lawn? Chihuahuas? Rainstorms?

This may be a useful exercise not least of all because it will force the writer to become aware of things about himself he may not have had cause to articulate until now.

Try to see whether the answers suggest any kind of narrative: If the writer says he's patient, ask him to give you an example of a situation when he demonstrated patience. Does he hate losing socks in the laundry because he's orderly? If so, on what other occasion did he demonstrate the same quality? Or perhaps he hates losing socks in the laundry because the nearest store that sells socks is 20 miles away. That's less of a character trait than a detail for the setting of a story, but it's all useful practice, as the writer is working his way toward writing just that. Use the writer's answer to come up with the next question, as in previous weeks.

After you've amassed a detailed portrait of the writer, pick half the answers and change them to create a new character. If the writer has blonde hair, give the new character black hair. If the writer loves astronomy, have the new characters like race cars. If the writer is a girl, make the character a boy. Here, again, be on the lookout for traits that could be expanded into small character narratives. Does the character love race cars because his father was a legendary driver who was killed on the course? And now the boy dreams of winning the race that eluded his father? If the character is a boy, and he has long hair, that's much more unusual than a girl with long hair. Perhaps the boy wears long hair because he likes a certain kind of music? Or, is it because in this town of 42 people, there is no barber? Each of these possibilities suggests a great deal of new detail toward a personality profile.

As you steer this imaginary character away from his inspiration—the writer himself—you could play the "or" game, as in the dress example above:

1. Is this person a long-haired person or a short-haired person?

2. Does she wear jeans or a dress?

3. Would this person prefer swimming in the lake or the ocean?

4. Does she enjoy eating pretzels or chips?

Some of these traits are less significant than others, but there's no reason not to have fun, and, besides, the more we know about our characters—even their junk-food preferences—the more clues we give ourselves as we broaden their personalities and search for story ideas. Maybe a character is obsessed with junk food and decides to quit it cold turkey for a month. Now that would be a story.

As a crowning challenge, you might "test-drive" this new character through several situations. That is, ask the writer, what would this person do if:

1. He saw someone cheating on a test?

2. He got lost in the woods?

3. He found out he had a long-lost brother?

Remind the writer that this character does not need to be a saint. Few people in life are. Characters appeal to audiences because they are as many-sided as human beings themselves; that is, noble in some situations, fearful in others, anxious in others. The whole point of creating characters is to liberate us from the censoring self-consciousness that comes into play when we are representing ourselves in writing: It's a "character"; it's not "you."

Mentor Materials

Section 3: Dialogue
Weeks 9–10

Week 9—Eavesdropping!

Purpose: To listen closely to the way people speak.

People speak very differently from the way they write. When we start writing, we become grammatical, formal, polished. When we speak, we're casual, self-revising, fragmentary, colloquial. Dialogue conveys spoken speech, not written speech, which is why it's so important for the writer to spend some time listening to the way people talk.

Help the writer by exposing her to new environments. Take her along on errands. Do something together you haven't done before, with the aim of listening to the people there speaking. Join her for the assignment by doing it yourself and comparing notes.

If the writer is stuck for ideas on whom to listen to, tell her to listen to everyone who's at the table for dinner, to listen during her favorite television program, or to listen to her friend as they speak on the phone.

In a sense, the assignment is merely a way to get the writer to listen closely to 20 conversations and to be reminded, from the perspective of a *writer*, just how informally dialogue works in real life. We'll be practicing creating it from scratch next week.

To review punctuation and dialogue tags, a line of dialogue should look like this:

"Blah blah blah," she said.

She said is the dialogue tag.

If you're following the model of a script, the dialogue would look like this:

>   Samantha: Blah blah blah.
>   John: Blah blah blah.

In a short story, the writer would use dialogue tags, not script form. For this assignment, though, either is acceptable.

Week 10—Creating dialogue

Purpose: To craft from scratch the kind of dialogue the writer overheard last week.

Help the writer by offering to play the role of the second character in a sample exchange. It's a fun opportunity to role-play.

If the writer is stuck, prompt him by asking what the second character might be feeling after what the first one just said. Would the first one's comment make the second one angry, suspicious, curious, wary? If the writer doesn't know how to begin, go to the 20 lines of dialogue from Week 9. Pick one, and have that be the first line of the exchange.

More broadly, you can take a break from the exercise and spend a little time "learning" more about each of the characters, beyond the 10 questions that were answered and 500 words that were written in Week 8. Alternatively, you can spend time elaborating on the situation in which the characters find themselves. If they're on the *Titanic*, what time of day is it? How cold is it? What part of the ship are they in? What did they have for their last meal? Etc. Answering more questions like this will give the writer more material to use in coming up with something for the characters to discuss.

Mentor Materials

Section 4: Observation
Weeks 11–12

Week 11—Who am I?

Purpose: To learn how to observe an object closely.

If the writer is stuck, you might take her through a sample exercise. Pick an object at home, even something as simple as a bookshelf or television, and ask 10 questions about it. In fact, it's even more useful to pick a mundane object; if the writer can come up with 10 things to say about a regular old bookshelf, imagine how much she'll be able to say about something more exciting.

As for the bookshelf, you can ask:

• How tall is it?
• How many shelves does it have?
• What color is it?
• From what material is it made?
• How many books does it contain?
• Is it new or old?
• How does the material feel to the touch?
• If it's made of wood, is it varnished?
• What are some of the books on its shelves?
• Is it dusty?

ANSWER TO RIDDLE: I am this book!

Week 12—The scene

Purpose: To observe a scene very closely.

Last week, the writer learned to describe a stationary object; this week, the challenge is to describe just as closely a more complicated tableau of moving parts.

Help the writer understand the difference between situation and scene. "Mom's relatives' visit for the weekend" is a situation; the conversation that takes place at the dinner table is a scene. Situations tend to be ongoing; scenes are finite. The situation is the context in which a scene happens; the scene is what happens.

When the writer was asked to come up with story ideas in the plot section, he was being asked to come up with *situations*: the background, the context, the setting, the things that are in place before the story begins. A retired farmer sets off on a cross-country drive to see an America he's never seen because he was too busy with farm work; a strike at the airplane hangar where the president is due to arrive the next day; a friendship between a woman who was alive in the 19th century and a girl who was born in the 21st—these are all *situations*. Scenes are one of the ways in which the story itself proceeds: a comical narration of the farmer navigating a complicated cloverleaf outside of a major urban center; the employees of the hangar breaking their tools as a symbol of their unhappiness; the elderly woman showing pictures to the girl—these are all *scenes*.

To help the writer find a scene on which to focus, look around. Scenes with interaction, or some kind of event, or even a minor narrative arc—returning his books to the library, Jimmy Constantine tries to sneak out before the late fines are assessed—work much better in a story (and might feature more detail for the writer to describe in this assignment), but the writer isn't yet creating a story. He's learning to pay attention to action. The woodchuck tap-tap-tapping away: That's action. The writer's brother practicing an instrument: That's action. The teller counting out change at the bank: That's action. So is the lightning splitting the sky, the cicadas making an evening ruckus, and Mom and Dad making dinner. As long as there's action, whether it's created by animate or inanimate objects, there's a scene for the writer to observe.

Mentor Materials

Section 5: Setting
Weeks 13–14

Week 13—Describing place

Purpose: To observe a place closely.

As in other sections, the setting section begins by providing training wheels for the imagination: asking the writer to riff on an existing place. (As in the character section, the writer will go on to invent a place from scratch next week.

Places are all around us. The lake is a place, and even though it looks still, anyone with the patience to observe it for an hour will discover that it's quite active, what with all the birds skidding about, animals making noise, and the wind rippling the water. The grocery store is a place: shoppers maneuvering their shopping carts (a writer might compare it to a go-kart track), acquaintances running into each other, the butcher packing the display case with fresh meat (what cuts and from what animal?). Even the kitchen at home is a place where meals are constantly being cooked, homework done, phone calls taken, daydreams indulged out the window, shopping lists drawn up, etc.

You can ask the writer to draw up a list of every place she can recall visiting over the last week. Ask which place she enjoyed the most (or least), and why. You can give her the option of recreating that place from memory, or visiting it once more, if that's a possibility. The writer should spend at least one hour in observation of the place in question, notebook in hand, jotting down even the smallest details.

The idea in this assignment is to try to see a familiar place with new eyes. Direct observation is likely to yield much fresher details than memory. When we use our memories, we tend to recall the most obvious, stereotypical details of a setting. At the town soccer field, we remember the goals, the green grass, the white lines separating the field. But if we actually visit the field, we notice that one of the goals has a huge rip in the corner, soccer balls constantly sailing through it. And the grass, while technically green, looks almost blue at a certain time of day. And the person who was drawing the white lines on the field must have slipped up because there's a funny squiggle right at the edge of the penalty box! Direct observation helps us notice idiosyncrasies rather than conventions.

But the idea isn't only to see closely. It's also to notice things differently. We visit our own kitchen so often that it becomes invisible to us. But if the writer can ask her siblings and parents to pretend she's invisible for an hour as she parks herself with a notebook in the corner, she will begin to notice all sorts of things that simply flew by her before. Only a writer paying close attention as an "invisible" being will notice her mother pausing at the dishes and staring for a moment out the window above the sink, leading to a note in the writer's notebook: "The kitchen is a place of daydreams."

Week 14—Inventing a country

Purpose: To learn how to describe an imagined place.

The Week 6 exercise on historical characters got the writer to learn about history alongside writing. This exercise does the same for geography and politics.

If the writer is stuck, help by providing a symbol and asking, "What could this stand for?" Or you could provide the aspect of the country that the symbol stands for and instruct the writer to "draw a symbol to represent this."

Having to define the symbol is a way of turning an abstraction into something concrete, something writers—whether of fiction or poetry—have to do a lot. In fact, we'll be doing more of this in the poetry section. Here, it's a gateway to using the imagination to populate a country from scratch—not unlike what an author has to do when he fills a blank page with a description of a setting.

If the writer is stuck trying to answer the 10 questions, ask him what the answer would be if he was answering for his country, be it the U.S., the U.K., Canada, etc. Now, just as in the character section, pick half the answers and change them for the country in question. For instance:

1. If Americans like to eat hamburgers, pizza, and ice cream, the citizens of Country X like to eat vegetables, soup, and fruit. Or frogs' legs, pig snouts,

and liver candies! Or oxygen, potassium, and magnesium in pure form! (A good chemistry lesson, by the way.) Note that the foods don't have to be "real" (e.g., "liver candies").

2. If America is friendly to Ugadougou (an invented nation, though it *is* the real world capital of Burkina Faso), then the citizens of Country X are not. Don't leave it there; ask why. This will force the writer to come up with a story. The Ugadougouans may have invaded Country X, making off with all the jewelry and children. Or the Ugadougouans may have simply beaten Country X in the competition to host the next Winter Olympics, a travesty because Ugadougou is a tropical country and Country X sits in snowbound mountains!

3. The geography of America is diverse: There are plains and mountains, lakes and oceans, cold places and warm places. Country X, then, isn't diverse. Let's say it's made entirely of desert. Or, if we're being consistent with the answer in #2, it snows there 300 days out of the year because it's the highest inhabited place on earth.

An added challenge in this exercise is to come up with answers that are consistent. So it's unlikely that the citizens of Country X eat a lot of vegetables and fruit (Answer #1) if they live 14,000 feet in the air! What do they eat, then? (These kinds of questions can lead to all sorts of interesting research projects, such as learning about the diets of the indigenous Indians who live in the highlands of Peru.)

Use the writer's answers to guide him toward a more–and–more detailed and consistent narrative about what his invented country is like.

Mentor Materials

Section 6: Point of View
Weeks 15–17

Week 15—Point of view

Purpose: To learn the difference between first-person and third-person narration.

Point of view is one of the most subtle and complex aspects of writing fiction. It has to do with who's telling the story (first-person vs. third-person); with whether the narrator's motives are influencing the telling of the story; and with how a narrator's general condition (e.g., misanthropic, naïve, self-deluding, etc.) affects the way the story is told, and so on.

Even the simple issue of who's telling the story isn't simple at all. If an "I" narrator is telling a story, that's likely to mean that the narrator is part of the events of the story. (Think about it: How many stories or novels have you read where an "I" narrator isn't somehow involved in the story?) An "I" narrator is also unlikely to know the goings-on of any character's mind nearly as well as his own. The reader is therefore locked into the perspective of this character, for better and worse. As the reader determines for himself whether this narrator is trustworthy, he must decide how skeptically to view his telling of the story.

A third-person narrator functions according to a different set of rules. With a third-person narrator, readers aren't as locked in as they are with a first-person narrator. An omniscient third-person narrator will be able to report with equal authority from the mind of every character. (Though this doesn't make him any more trustworthy.) A *limited omniscient* narrator will tell the story from the perspective of one of the characters in the story, keeping close to that character's viewpoint at all times, and rarely straying to visit the minds of the other characters.

These are complicated concepts, and they won't form a part of the writer's practice this week. However, it's important for you to understand at this stage just how much point of view affects what can be revealed in a story and how.

This week, the writer's work will consist of not much more than switching "he" to "I" or vice versa. But even this presents an opportunity to ask the writer some questions that may prepare him for the point-of-view lessons to come:

If the writer is switching to first-person:

1. To whom might this character be providing this information?
2. Which details do you think he would add or take out if he was saying all this to his mother? To a woman he's courting? To his boss? To an enemy?
3. How well do you think he understands what his mother thinks about things? His wife? His boss? His enemy?

If the writer is switching to third-person:

1. Who's giving us all this information about this person?
2. How well does she know her? *How* do they know each other?
3. If she is a friend, is she giving us an overly flattering portrait? If a foe, an overly unfair one?

Week 16—Point of view (motive)

Purpose: To think about how a story changes depending on the interests of whoever is telling it.

The point of this exercise is to accustom the writer to motive in storytelling. We want him to approach characters critically: What stake does this or that character have in the outcome of this story? Is this influencing the way he or she is telling the story, what they're revealing and when? Especially if the writer is writing a scene for the lesson from scratch, he should give some thought to what his characters want, and how to make that clear in the story.

If the writer is stuck, assign him one of the two roles in one of the exchanges. You take the other and start the debate. If you've chosen scenario #2 (John and Sylvia), you could say:

Sylvia: Mom, John trampled the flowers, not me!

Mom: John, what do you have to say to that?

John: She's saying that because I wouldn't let her practice my oboe. I was riding my bike around there, but I didn't trample the flowers!

Mom: John, you know you're on probation. With the grades you've been bringing home, you're begging for a grounding. You're lucky I let you ride the bike outside at all.

John: Mom, I didn't do it! Sylvia was playing catch with the dog, throwing the tennis ball from the porch. That's how it must have happened.

Sylvia: Poochie didn't go anywhere near the bushes! You know only one of us is going to get to go to the concert next week, so you're setting me up!

Dad [walking in]: What's all this commotion? By the way, honey, I'm *really* sorry. I wasn't looking and I backed the car into the flowerbed. The good news is I was on my way to Lowe's. I promise I'll buy some replacements!

Week 17—Point of view (mood)

Purpose: To learn how a story changes depending on the mood of the narrator.

To help the writer understand the way mood affects perception, ask her to remember the last time she was in a funk. Did it make her listless and indifferent when the dog tried to cuddle? Was she irritable when you asked for help and pessimistic when you said things would get better? Ask her to remember a time of joy; was she energetic and inquiring, volunteering to help with the cake? Did the very same things that made her annoyed when she was upset—like the cuddling dog—suddenly bring joy?

The first task here is to pick an object that the two characters in very different moods will observe. This task should be familiar from the object-observation exercise (Week 11). What object (or, for that matter, scene, as in Week 12) might appear different to two people in very different moods? Well, a still, unpeopled lake at sunset may seem romantic to one person and desolate to another. The optimistic person may be there with his or her spouse, and he may be viewing the lake from the porch of a cozy and secluded lakeside inn. The pessimist may be viewing it from the opening of a wet tent during a thunderstorm. (Of course, a lot depends on the personalities of these individuals. Some people *like* wet tents during a thunderstorm.)

Once you've settled on an object or scene, help the writer come up with a mood or personality likely to see in this object/scene something negative. Ask: What kind of person might not be very happy to be in the presence of this?

What might have happened to put this person in this mood? Was this person expecting to find something else here? Then do the same for a character likely to see something positive in the same object/scene: Is the person satisfied because he was looking for this object/scene? Or is it that he's a systematic optimist? Why was he looking for the object/scene? Answering questions like these will help the writer build up a situation or narrative around the individual's interaction with the object/scene, which, in turn, will help populate the description she's been asked to write.

This exercise is more challenging than many of its predecessors in that it asks the writer to compose her answer not as a series of notes, but as a piece of fiction. The difference between the two may seem negligible at this point, since the exercise asks the writer to compose her answer as straight forward description. (The first challenge exercise goes further.) But as we draw toward the end of the fiction course and move into the next level of this series, we're going to be shifting from the practice of writing skills to actual writing in this way more and more.

Mentor Materials

Section 7: Writing a Short Story from Scratch
Weeks 18

Prior to the start of this week's exercise, review with the writer the basics of the sections they've studied this year: Plot, Character, Dialogue, Setting, Point of View. Review the basics of what makes a compelling plot (suspense, a character's quest). You may wish to revisit the writer's exercises for that section as well, in case there's a story idea there that the writer would like to use for this week's story.

Then proceed to the character lessons. The writer has experience drawing a character from scratch. Who will be the characters of this week's story? The writer may follow the example of Week 8 and draw up a list of characteristics about himself, half of which he will alter for this imaginary character (in keeping with the demands of the story idea), or he may take a shortcut and draw the new character (and whoever else will appear in the story) directly.

Dialogue: If the writer knows who will speak to whom and when the dialogue will happen, he may wish to practice dialogue between those two characters at the outset. If not, he can pause and practice right at the moment he arrives at dialogue in his story.

Before starting, the writer should think about where the story is taking place (setting) and who's telling it (point of view). Even if the physical setting won't play a large role in the story, the writer may be surprised by how useful he will find an hour's worth of observation prep before the story. As for point of view, spend some time discussing how the story might change depending on who's telling it. If the story is about how a group of miners survived underground for 33 days and the narrator is one of the miners, speaking in the first-person, he will have very limited knowledge of what happened above ground during the time of his entrapment (unless he explains to us that he asked those who were above ground or read newspaper accounts; this, however, requires that the story be told after the rescue, removing one ingredient of suspense. See how interrelated the details of craft are?). If the narrator is all-knowing and third-person, he can float between the mine and the aboveground rescue operation without obstruction.

This kind of quick refresher is likely to give the writer some much-needed tools to rely on as he begins the challenging but noble task of filling a blank page.

PART II

POETRY

Section 1:
Introduction to Poetry

(or, I'm a poet and I don't know it)

Weeks 1–2

Week 1

The alphabet exercise

Purpose: To begin to understand the difference between fiction and poetry.

What's poetry, anyway? Instinctively, we know what poems look like, but can you put into words how poems are different from short stories? Let's come up with a couple of things that are true for poems, but not true for stories:

1. The lines in poems are usually much shorter than the lines in stories
2. Poems are organized in groups of lines (called stanzas)
3. Sometimes, poems rhyme
4. Poems are (usually) much shorter than stories
5. Poems have many more restrictions than stories (some poems have to rhyme; others have to have a certain number of syllables in each line, or a certain number of lines in each stanza; etc.)
6. This may be hard to appreciate now, but poetry *sounds* very different from fiction. Because poems must pack their meaning into a far smaller space, using far fewer words than fiction, they end up sounding a lot more charged and intense than short stories. The language in short stories often resembles the language people use in everyday life. Less so in poetry.

These characteristics, among others, make poetry very different from fiction. Think of poetry and prose as distant cousins, or, better yet, two artisans who use the same material—words—to make very different objects. Poetry presents an excitingly different creative challenge from fiction. If, until now, you've found yourself drawn only to fiction, give poetry a try. I used to focus only on fiction, but then had to teach a college writing course that included poetry as well. I'm so grateful for that forced introduction because it brought me into a new world of words that has made me not only interested in poetry, but a far better fiction writer, too.

Part of the reason for this has to do with something mentioned above: Poems have far less room and far fewer words than stories to make their point. Poems tend to deploy more precise and expressive words, images, and ideas, as these have to do that much more work in presenting an idea or feeling to the reader. The language of poetry is especially concentrated. Think of it as a balloon inflated to the fullest, a single breath away from exploding.

Part of what makes poems different is all the restrictions poets work under. This week, you'll write a whole poem while working under one such restriction: each new line of your poem must begin with the next letter of the alphabet.

In a page of your notebook, line the left margin with the alphabet, like this:

A _____
B _____
C _____
D _____
E _____
F _____
G _____
H _____
I _____
J _____
K _____
L _____
M_____
N _____
O _____
P _____
Q _____
R _____
S _____
T _____
U _____
V _____
W_____
X _____
Y _____
Z _____

Now, let's try to tell a story where each new line begins with a new letter of the alphabet. In each line, you can write **complete sentences** or **fragments**. Here are examples of both:

Complete sentences:

A screeching noise woke me up.
Before I got up, I looked at the alarm clock.
Crazy, I thought: It's not even 5:00 a.m.
Downstairs, everything was quiet.
Everyone still seemed to be sleeping.
Funny things happen in the night while everyone sleeps.

Fragments:

Anyway,
Brothers and sisters
Can
Do
Everything together like
Friends

(Sometimes, it's okay to give yourself a hand by using a "throwaway" word like "anyway," just to help you get going.)

This exercise actually has two restrictions: 1) you have to choose words that make some kind of sense for the story you're telling *and* 2) they ought to be words that begin with the appropriate letter. Therefore, you may wish to do a **practice round** that has no restrictions. Just write the first five words that start with A that come to mind, then the first five words that start with B, and so on. Hopefully, this will warm up your "vocabulary muscles" and make it easier to come up with a story for the real exercise.

When you're ready for your alphabet poem: Try to tell a single story throughout the exercise. If you're stuck, you could keep going with the strange-noise-downstairs story in the first example. You could tell the story of a horse who can talk (A Brown Colt Dances, Explains Facts, Grabs my Hand...) or pirates attacking a ship (A ship appeared on the horizon,/a Black flag waving from its mast./The Captain ordered the sailors to clear/the Deck.) The story doesn't have to make perfect sense, and it's fine to help yourself by inserting a "help-word" such as "a" or "the" before an alphabet letter:

A ship appeared on the horizon,

a Black flag waving from its mast.
The Captain ordered the sailors to clear
the Deck.

It's also acceptable to alternate complete **clauses** (the first three lines in the pirate story above) with fragments (the fourth). (A clause is a group of words that includes both a noun and a verb. "The brown colt dances" is a clause, but "the brown colt" is not.)

Modified exercise: If the 26-letter alphabet feels like too much, forget about the last 13 letters. Just try to get to M.

Challenge exercises:

1. Write an alphabet poem backwards, with your first line beginning with Z and your last line with A.

2. Get as far as you can in an alphabet poem where each new line has only one word.

Week 2

Acronym poem

Purpose: Write a poem where each new line begins not with the next letter of the alphabet but with the next letter of an acronym (ASAP, TTYL, CIA).

This week, you'll use an acronym to help you write your second poem.

Acronyms are abbreviations of words using their first letters. ASAP is an acronym for "*a*s *s*oon *a*s *p*ossible"; CIA stands for Central Intelligence Agency.

Your job in this lesson is to come up with 10 mini-poems where each new line begins with the next letter of an acronym. (So, you'll have to start by coming up with 10 acronyms.) I'll give you the first five acronyms; you'll have to come up with the rest.

My five:
  AWOL (*a*bsent *w*ithout *l*eave)
  FWIW (*f*or *w*hat *i*t's *w*orth)
  ANFSCD (*a*nd *n*ow *f*or *s*omething *c*ompletely *d*ifferent)
  LSHMBH (*l*aughing *s*o *h*ard *m*y *b*elly *h*urts)
  AARP (*A*merican *A*ssociation of *R*etired *P*ersons)

The same rules apply as for the alphabet poem—both complete sentences and fragments are fine; so are both complete and incomplete clauses. For instance, for AWOL, you could do:

  Always
  Want to have
  One more
  Lollipop

Try hard for your poem to make sense instead of being a random collection of words.

Challenge exercises:

1. Come up not with mini-poems but new *acronyms* using the same letters. For instance, you could revise AWOL to stand for:

    > Arbitrary
    > Withdrawal
    > Of
    > Lollipops

2. Write mini-poems (that make sense) using first letters not of an alphabet or acronym but of words:

    > 1. JURASSIC
    > 2. SUPERCOLLIDER
    > 3. EXTRAORDINARY
    > 4. MASSIVE
    > 5. PIPELINE

3. Write mini-poems (that make sense) using not first letters but first *words*, drawn from common phrases:

    For instance:
    > Over
    > My
    > Dead
    > Body

    could become something like:

    > Over the moon I sailed,
    > My chariot aiming heavenward while the world slept like
    > Dead people, my
    > Body becoming lighter and lighter.

    Here are five you could try:
    > 1. This Is Ground Control
    > 2. Roses are Red and Violets are Blue
    > 3. Fairy Tales Can Come True
    > 4. And They Lived Happily Ever After
    > 5. Out Of Sight, Out Of Mind

4. Write mini-poems (that make sense) where each new line begins with a
    new *random* word rather than part of a phrase:

    1. Iron Broccoli Gem Squirrel Platoon India Racecar
    2. Recycle Underslept Windy Magic Snap Burrow Upset
    3. America Baseball Charlie Diana Everyone Fantasy Glowing
    4. Spoon Sleep Milk Bib Snow Cute
    5. Poem Poem Poem Poem Poem Poem

Section 2:
Description

Weeks 3–6

Week 3

As unhappy as a bluefish at the end of a fishing line: Comparisons

Purpose: To learn how to use similes and metaphors.

Imagine if someone said, "It snowed." Could you picture in your mind what that person was telling you? Probably—most of us know what snow looks like. Now, imagine if that person said, "It snowed so much that going to the mailbox felt like walking through water." We've all probably waded through a pool or an ocean, so now, we're not only imagining the snow with our minds but also *feeling* with our bodies what walking through that snow must have been like. That second impression—the comparison of walking through the snow to walking through water—helps us to imagine more richly how much snow there was.

There are lots of ways to compare one thing to another, but this week, we're going to focus on two: **similes** and **metaphors**.

A simile compares two things by putting one thing next to another, using words such as "like" or "as." For example, "The rising sun looked **like** an apple on fire." Metaphors, on the other hand, compare two things by saying that one thing *is* another. "The rising sun **was** an apple on fire." Clearly, metaphors don't mean this literally but poetically. Both similes and metaphors help us imagine what something is like by comparing it to something else.

How does one come up with a simile or a metaphor? Let's use my example from above: I started with the snow. The aspect of it I wanted to highlight in the comparison was how much of it there was and how difficult it made walking. If I wanted to emphasize the *size* of a snowbank using a comparison, I would have tried to think of tall things and said something like: "The snowbank was a skyscraper towering above Mom's Mazda." If I wanted to focus on how *cold* the snow made it, I would have tried to think of other

cold things and said something like: "The snow made it as cold as an icebox." But since I wanted to focus on what it *felt* like to walk through the snow, I had to come up with another image having to do with sensation. Wading through snow is all about fighting through resistance; what else feels like that, I wondered. Doing sit-ups might work, I thought, but that wasn't a very precise comparison. With snow you're trying to move forward; with sit-ups, you're more or less stationary. Maybe there was a better image, an image having to do with movement and resistance? That's when I remembered what it feels like to wade through water.

For this week's assignment, you'll complete 10 fill-in-the-blank exercises that practice your knack for these kinds of comparisons. Let's do the first couple together so you can observe how I come up with the comparisons.

1. As excited as a _____.

    Process: I start by thinking: Who or what exhibits excitement? Lottery winners exhibit excitement. Students having finished their homework for the day exhibit excitement. Moms who've just been told their children have finished their homework for the day (and cleaned up their room) exhibit excitement. And there you have it: As excited as a student who just finished her homework. Or: As excited as a mom whose daughter has finished her homework.

Challenge question:
Is this a simile or metaphor?

Now come up with your own answer: As excited as who or what?

2. John had told Sam, over and over: no visitors in the woodshop. But Sam seemed to pay attention about as well as a _____.

    Process: The first couple of sentences here are just for information. Our focus goes immediately to the last sentence. What are we seeing there? Sam doesn't pay attention well. The assignment asks us to compare Sam to something else that fidgets or is restless or can't focus. What about:

    But Sam seemed to pay attention about as well as a hummingbird.

Challenge question:
Simile or metaphor?

Now come up with your own answer. What did Sam pay attention about as well as?

3. Charlie gazed at the men moving around on the baseball diamond as if they were _____.

Process: This is a tricky one. The first thing to do is to determine for what we're trying to find a comparison. For Charlie? For the baseball diamond? No—for the men on it; the sentence says "as if *they* were..." This comparison implies that Charlie was mesmerized by the baseball players. What kind of individuals might transfix us as viewers? What about magicians? Or something more fanciful, like special emissaries who are telling us the secret of our future? So, how about:

Charlie gazed at the men moving around the baseball diamond as if their feet were writing out the secret meaning of his life.

Challenge question:
Simile or metaphor?

Now come up with your own answer. What were the men moving around like?

Finish the rest of these on your own:

4. The apple was as green as a _____.
5. The yacht bobbed in the vast blue sea, nothing more than a _____.
6. Whenever Meredith couldn't figure her way out of a quandary, she ran. Miles and miles. It helped her clear her head. Streaking down the carriageways of the woods around her home, she felt like a _____.
7. Threading a needle is like _____.
8. He was a _____; he never let disappointment get to him.
9. The cat slunk around in the darkness, a_____.
10. The stars studded the sky, a _____.

Challenge exercises:

1. Come up with five similes and five metaphors on your own.
2. Find five similes and five metaphors in today's newspaper. (They're all over the place—trust me.)

Week 4

Abstract into concrete

Purpose: To come up with concrete words for abstract objects and ideas.

In both fiction and poetry, it's much better to use concrete images than abstract ideas.

What's the difference? Abstract is anything that means something different depending on who's hearing about it. Love is abstract—whoever comes across the word thinks of a different thing. (You might be thinking about your mom darning one of your socks and I may be thinking of a dozen flowers.) Darned socks and flowers are both concrete; when I say flowers, you're not going to think of a refrigerator. Neither will anyone else hearing the word (unless they're really strange). You might say, yes, but there are lots of different kinds of flowers, and you'd be right. There's a way to be even more concrete here: azaleas, tulips, mums, rhododendrons. Put another way—and you might remember this distinction from your "Who Am I?" exercise from the fiction section—abstract is general and concrete is specific.

Concrete is better than abstract because concrete is a lot easier to imagine— it's clear *exactly* what has to be imagined. (And when we read books, we have to imagine everything, as the book itself is nothing but a bunch of ink on a page.) If a reader has to lose time and get distracted by figuring out what exact kind of love the writer is referring to—sock-darning, or flower-giving, or the million other kinds?—he's liable to get frustrated and stop reading the piece in front of him. This week's exercise is all about figuring out how to make abstract things concrete through specific descriptions.

Let's start by thinking of some abstract things, shall we? Let's include love. Can you think of others? Take a moment to jot down 5. If you're stuck, look at my list:

1. Love
2. Anger
3. Generosity

4. Blue
5. Five

You'll notice that the first three are emotions, but #4 is a color and #5 is a number. Colors are abstractions. Blue is an abstraction; "blue cat" is not. And numbers like "five" are abstractions, too; "five fingers" is not. It's the concrete details that turn an abstraction into something very easy to visualize, because it's so specific.

Another great way to test for concrete vs. abstract, if you're stuck, is to ask: Can you pour chocolate sauce on it? It's not a foolproof test, but it generally works. Can you pour chocolate sauce on blue? No. On a blue cat? Yes!

So, this week, your job will be to write five mini-poems (four lines each) describing abstract things in concrete terms. (You can use my list, or your own.) So, for instance, if you were writing a poem about love, it could look something like this:

> Love is a hand reaching for another hand,
> A warm bed on a cold night,
> A ship sailing toward the harbor,
> A grin on a face at the arrival gate.

This may remind you a little of the comparison exercise from last week: You're comparing one thing to another. (Quick: Do the above lines consist of metaphor or simile?) The difference is that you're translating something abstract into something concrete.

Challenge exercises:

1. Write an alphabet poem where each line describes the shape of its starting letter in concrete terms. (A is a man doing jumping jacks...)

2. Do the same thing for a number poem ("1 is a telephone pole, 2 is a swan...")

Week 5

Colors into words

Purpose: To compose a poem of concrete images about an abstract painting.

The painter Mark Rothko, who died in 1970, is probably best known for paintings that seem to be divided into a series of lines or boxes. These boxes appear to consist of a single solid color, though if you look more closely, they don't exactly. (You can get a good introduction to Rothko's work on Wikipedia.)

For an idea of what I mean, consider Rothko's "Untitled (Black on Grey)," painted late in his life.

Turn to the back cover of this book, and you'll see the painting in full color, although the only colors are shades of black and white.

Rothko's painting is pure abstraction. (In fact, painters like him were officially known as "abstract expressionists," though Rothko himself didn't think the title fit him very well. You might notice that abstraction is a lot more effective in art than it is in writing.)

Your job this week will be to write a poem filled with concrete images about this painting. This week's poem will be longer than last week's mini-poems. Set yourself a goal of 20 lines. This week's assignment may remind you of the photo-into-a-story exercise from the fiction section: You have to "translate" an image with few clues about its meaning into a more or less coherent narrative.

What might a poem like this look like? Start by spending a couple of minutes looking at the painting. Do something else and then look at it again. If you can do other homework for a couple of hours and then return to the painting once more, do that. Throughout, make notes about what pops into your mind when you're looking at the painting. How does it make you feel? What kind of mood does it put you in? What does it remind you of? You'll really have to use your imagination because, well, it looks like a black box on top of a gray box! But you might notice that the black box is bigger, and that the grey box, especially, isn't solidly grey. If you look closely, you'll see all kinds of white brushstrokes that made me think of feathers, which, in turn, made me think of the sky....

Start by filling a page in your notebook with thoughts and musings about the painting. These will provide material for your 20-line poem, when you are ready to move on to it. Don't worry about whether these observations are "correct" or not; write down whatever comes to mind. Just know that in the poem, you're going to have to use only concrete images. So if your notes include an observation like "this poem makes me scared," that's fine for your observations, but it won't be good enough for your poem. You'll need to "convert" the abstract idea of being scared into a concrete image. You can do that in one of several ways, for instance by describing the fear as a physical object ("I feel like the black box is inside me, a crow unfurling its wings..." or "the painting is a black crow unfurling its wings over my eyes...").

You could focus on the experience of viewing the painting; you can write about how it affected your mood throughout the day, whether you thought of it even after you were done with your homework; and, finally, you could, of course, write a poem about what you think the painting's *about*.

When you've finished writing your observations, take a break—an hour, a day, even two days. Then return to your notebook page. Use the phrases and sentences you've put down there as a starting place for your 20-line poem. The poem can be made up of those lines (as long as they're concrete)—or you can add new ones. You can also write *all* new lines, of course. Your poem can rhyme, or not. It can contain complete sentences, or not. It can be divided into stanzas, or not. The one requirement for this poem is that it use at least one concrete image to express how you feel about the painting.

Challenge exercises:

1. Write an expanded version of the poem you wrote last week, where each of the 20 lines "translates" "Black on Grey" into something concrete. The basis of comparison could be the colors (black, grey), the shapes (two rectangles), the line between them (as is my focus below), or a mix:

   "Black on Grey" is the horizon in a world bleached of blue,
   The end of the world outside my airplane window,
   the line of the sea on a wintertime day,
   the line between nighttime and dawn.

2. Look up a different kind of abstract expressionist image (Google "abstract expressionism" or, for a specific choice, "Jackson Pollock") and write a poem about it.

Week 6

Going where no man has gone

Purpose: To use our imagination to envision invisible things.

Creative writing is about things that aren't easily visible—unusual ways to say something, or getting inside the heads of invented (but interesting and believable) characters. All this depends on imagination. This exercise forces you to use yours, because it's all about going inside things that aren't very easily accessible, physically speaking—a stone, a brain, a rain droplet. You will need to imagine what the inside of some object looks, feels, tastes, smells, or sounds like. Then you'll have to write a poem (20 lines) about what you saw when you went there. Just make sure you choose one that's truly hard to get inside. Here's an example:

The inside of a question mark
is slippery and damp.
No way to climb to the top without
slipping down the back or the side.

And then what? Lots of climbing.
Of course you can take the ferry to
The Dot.
The Tasmania to the Australia of the rest (if you will).

I was in a coffee shop one time, and some smart-aleck says:
"So which is the question, which the mark?"
I smacked him with a comma.

But when I went home, I thought and thought:
What do you call the two parts of a question mark?
A grammatical identity crisis (if you will).
Were we one nation, or like North and South Korea?

I called up the exclamation mark, the colon, and the quotes.
We debated all night

While the dash, the period, and the comma laughed from a corner.
This case remains open (if you will).

This cheeky little poem doesn't really imagine what the *inside* of a question mark looks *like*. Instead, it considers the question mark as a physical shape. It looks like a water slide, doesn't it? Hence the slipping and sliding mentioned in the first **stanza**. And after you've gone to the bottom, the only way back up is by climbing. Then I remembered that the question mark consists of two parts—the curve and the dot. That got me thinking about what they might be separated by. Water, I decided. (Why not?) That, in turn made me think of Australia and Tasmania, which are part of one nation, but are separated by a body of water.

Do you remember what a line like "The Tasmania to the Australia of the rest (if you will)" is called? The right answer is **metaphor**. A metaphor is a direct comparison that does not use "like" or "as." The curve is Australia (roughly speaking) and the dot is Tasmania. The correlation is between a bigger thing and a smaller thing that belong to a single unit (the country of Australia, in one case, and the question mark, in the other). Lines like "A grammatical identity crisis (if you will)" and "This case remains open (if you will)" are also metaphorical: they compare grammar to an identity crisis and an outstanding question to an open police case, respectively.

Mentioning Australia got me wondering what the two parts of a question mark are officially called. I had no idea. So I decided to riff on that. And so forth.

An important note which should recall the dialogue exercise (Week 10 in the Fiction section) where a fifth-grader named Samantha was speaking to a dog: I didn't plan out what I would write. I made the starting choice of what to focus on (the physical shape of the question mark) and simply went from there, each line giving me an idea for the next.

You can pick anything to which we don't have easy access. You could go shooting around inside a spark, diving through all the little pores in a piece of coral, or mountain climbing inside the stem of a flower. You can go inside a chef's hat (called a toque) like the lead character in "Ratatouille" (Is the chef bald? Did he wash his hair this morning?), or inside the scone he is baking in the oven (Pretty warm, eh?). You could go inside an engine and have some fun with the speed of a vehicle. You can go inside the mind of a friend and figure out what she's thinking. When you get to these places, answer the questions posed by the Five Senses:

What does it look like?
How does it smell?
How does it taste?
What does it feel like?
What does it sound like?

You may not be able to answer each question for each destination, but they are a good starting point. Imagine you're an explorer writing a guidebook to a place no one's been before. What did you do there and what would you tell us about it?

Challenge exercise:

Instead of going inside an object, go inside an experience you've never had. Write a poem about what it would be like to land on Mars, or, closer to home, work the graveyard shift as a watchman at a factory. There are ways you can get ideas for your poem, of course: You can do some research about Mars on the Web; you can find a factory watchman and interview him. Whether you do is up to you. Research can get our imaginations started, but for this exercise, it isn't essential. You already have more notions about Mars and factory watchmen than you know.

Section 3:
Getting the Words Right

Weeks 7–11

Week 7

Synonyms, antonyms, homonyms

Purpose: To learn how to use synonyms, antonyms, and homonyms.

As I mentioned in the introduction to the poetry section, every word counts for much more in poetry than in a short story. An average poem might have no more than a couple of hundred words, whereas a short story will usually have a couple of thousand. So in a poem, each word must accomplish as much as 10 words in a short story! And we have to choose our words with that much more care and attention. It helps to know vocabulary, and it helps to know semantic relationships between words. **Semantic** means anything having to do with meaning. We'll practice that this week by learning about synonyms, antonyms, and homonyms.

Synonyms are words that mean more or less the same thing as another word. "Happy" and "joyful"; "festive" and "merry/celebratory"; "throw" and "hurl" are all synonym pairs. Adjectives can be synonyms; so can verbs, nouns, and other parts of speech.

Antonyms are words that mean the opposite: "Empty" and "full"; "fast" and "slow"; "loud" and "quiet" are antonym pairs.

Homonyms are words that are pronounced the same way but don't necessarily have the same spelling, and mean different things. Think of "your" and "you're," "there" and "their," "bear" and "bare." Homonyms *can* be spelled the same; think of "spruce" (noun; a kind of tree) and "spruce" (verb; to tidy up).

This exercise has two parts.

Part 1a: Come up with a synonym for each of the following five words. These words are a mix of adjectives (1–3), a verb (4), and a noun (5). There's a special challenge with 4 and 5: Even though the originals are similar, their synonyms probably won't be.

1. Bright

2. Annoying
3. Delicious
4. Complain
5. Complaint

Part 1b: Antonyms: You know the drill.
1. Extinguish
2. Paralysis
3. Break
4. Whiny
5. Delicious

Part 1c: Homonyms: How many can you come up with for each entry?
1. Aisle
2. Idol
3. Buy
4. Holy
5. Road

Part 2:
Your turn. Pick five words and find five synonyms; pick another five and come up with five antonyms; come up with five homonym pairs. (You'll get bonus points if it's a triplet or even a quartet rather than a pair. They exist!)

Challenge exercise:

Look up each of the assigned words in 1a and 1b in a thesaurus (also possible at thesaurus.com) and familiarize yourself with all the words listed there. A thesaurus is a handy tool for a writer.

Week 8

If I could count the ways

Purpose: To practice making the same point in many different ways.

Last week, you familiarized yourself with synonyms. This week, you're going to practice synonym *sentences*. Your job here will be to come up not with a word that means close to the same thing as another, but a whole *sentence* whose meaning is similar to another's.

Your first task is to come up with a sentence—any sentence, about anything. It shouldn't be too long or too short, just an ordinary everyday sentence.
Here's an example:

> Even though it was raining, I went for a bike ride—
> and regretted it later.

The next step is to rewrite the sentence in 10 different ways, using as few of the same words as possible—that is, you'll be using lots of synonyms—but preserving the general meaning. It's fine to diverge from the basic meaning a little, and it's okay to use some of the same words. You can switch around parts of the sentence. You can also make your new sentences funny or silly or nonsensical or fragments. Examples, based on the sentence above:

1. Water dropped from the heavens, but I cycled anyway, and rued it.
2. The firmament sparkled with wetness, but there I was on two wheels, two hours away from a nasty cold.
3. A waterfall from the sky. I am a biped. Soon, I will need NyQuil®.
4. Buckets of water descending from the clouds, I spun the spokes of my chariot, right into a fever.
5. I would hate myself for having bicycled in a monsoon.
6. A torrent of droplets pounding my shoulders, my tires kissing the pavement, the flu knocking on the door of my head.
7. Rain. Bicyclist. Sore throat.

8. As the atmosphere dumped its favorite liquid, I pushed the aluminum frame further and further, a forest of pain growing inside my head.

9. It trickles and pours, but I am on twin windmills, as a cough rattles my chest.

10. A downpour, a wannabe Lance Armstrong, a trip to the clinic.

Notice that I left myself a bit of wiggle room in the third fact communicated by the sentence—"… and regretted it later." That could mean a lot of things: a cold, a ruined bike, something else. You can give yourself a leg up in the same way.

The real challenge is finding 10 ways of saying the same thing. You might do a side exercise of synonyms for some key concepts in the sentence. (In the case of my sentence that would have meant drawing up four columns: "Rainstorm," "Sky," "Bicycle," "Illness.") Try to go beyond literal pairings like sky = firmament. For the purposes of this exercise, sky could be "the air up there," "heavens," "clouds," "seven miles up," etc. In the same way, a bicycle could be a "chariot" or a "conveyance," or even a "spaceship," as long as it preserves the general idea of motion and its role in the sentence.

Challenge exercise:

Write 10 antonym sentences for your sentence.

Week 9

Crossword

Purpose: To look very, very closely at the letters that make up words.

Poetry sometimes demands closer attention than fiction. As we've discussed, having less room to make our point means we have to choose the perfect word. To choose the perfect word, we have to develop a feel for words that goes beyond meaning. Our sense of words must expand to include how they sound to us, how they look to us, what letters they share with other words (for echoes of sound), and so on. This week, we will use a crossword puzzle to get *really* up close and personal with words.

This week, your job will be to come up with 20 clues for 20 answers—10 down and 10 across—for a crossword puzzle that your mentor and friends (or parents and siblings) will then have to solve! See: it's not only you who has to do the work in this exercise book.

How to begin? You'll need three pieces of notebook paper: one where you will write down the clues your mentor and friends will use to guess the answers (notebook page A), one where you will draw empty boxes that your mentor and friends will have to fill in with the answers (notebook page B), and a sheet for yourself that has the answer boxes filled with the correct answers (notebook page C).

Let's begin together. I will take you through the first four clues and answers; feel free to use these in your own crossword puzzle, or if you want more of a challenge, start your own crossword from scratch.

WORD 1:

Step 1. Pick an answer. You should pick a long word, a word with lots of different letters, so that we have lots of letters to intersect with when we are choosing our second word. It could be a noun, verb, adjective, adverb, or another part of speech. It could be a person with a proper name (first and last names should be written as one word in the answer boxes) or an object. How about… "constitution"? That's a nice long word. Let's start by counting how many letters it has: 12. So, draw 12 boxes in the middle of notebook pages B and C with the number 1 in the upper left hand corner of the first box. (It doesn't matter whether you draw these boxes horizontally or vertically, but let's say we start horizontally.)

[1] CONSTITUTION

Fill the boxes in notebook page C—your personal answer sheet—with the word "constitution."

Step 2: We have to come up with a clue that will help your friends guess the answer. What's a good clue for "constitution?" You could say something like:

> Word 1 (Across): "The law of the land"
> or
> Word 1 (Across): "Created by The Founding Fathers"

Write this clue on notebook page A. Whoever's doing the puzzle will have to read the clue from that paper and then try to put the answer in the boxes you've drawn on notebook page B.

Okay, so we have all we need for the first of our 20 clues and answers: the clue on notebook page A, the empty boxes on page B, and the boxes with the answer filled in on page C. Let's move on to the second answer/clue.

The rules here are a little different. We have to come up with an answer that contains one of the letters in "constitution, so the words will overlap." Since we drew the boxes for "constitution" horizontally, we'll have to draw the boxes for this word vertically. Can you think of one? Before I provide you with a sample answer, write down five words—long words are best—that share at least one letter with constitution:

1.
2.
3.
4.
5.

WORD 2:

How about the word "determination"? It overlaps with "constitution" in quite a few places—the t's, the i's, o's, the n's—so we have many options for where the two words can intersect. Let's say we'll intersect the first t's in both words.

Step 1: "Determination" has 13 letters, so draw 13 boxes vertically on pages B and C (with the number 2 in the upper left-hand corner of the first box to indicate that this is our second word) where the third box in "deTermination" intersects with the fifth box in "consTitution" so that the answers, filled in, look like this:

```
                         2
                         D
                         E
          1 C O N S T I T U T I O N
                         E
                         R
                         M
                         I
                         N
                         A
                         T
                         I
                         O
                         N
```

As with the first word, fill in the answer only on page C, your personal answer sheet.

Step 2: We need a clue for "determination." We can describe someone who's very determined, or we can use a synonym. You'll remember that synonyms are words that mean more or less the same thing. So what means the same thing as "determination"? What about: perseverance? Or: dedication, persistence, resolve, purpose? Any of these words will do. Our clue could say:

Word 2 (Down): Synonym of perseverance

As with the first word, write this clue down on page A.

WORD 3:

Ready to pick our next answer? What about... "rambunctious"? Rambunctious shares letters with both "constitution" and "determination," so it's up to you where to intersect it, and also whether to draw the answer boxes (on pages B and C) vertically or horizontally. I chose to intersect it with the fifth letter in "deTermination", which is vertical, so I had to draw the boxes for "rambunctious" horizontally.

```
                              2
                              D
                              E
            1 C O N S T I T U T I O N
                              E
            3 R A M B U N C T I O U S
                              M
                              I
                              N
                              A
                              T
                              I
                              O
                              N
```

Remember to fill in the answer on page C.

Step 2: Since we've practiced synonyms, let's practice antonyms in our clue. You'll remember that antonyms are words that mean the opposite of another word. So, what would be the opposite of "rambunctious"? How about:

Word 3 (Across). Antonym of quiet, calm, silent, shy

Write the clue on page A.

Here's where the fun starts. Now, we have ourselves an opportunity to create a new word using two—rather than one—letters from previously used words. Choose two letters from two different words and see if you can come up with a third word that has the same letters the same distance apart. For instance, take the third "t" in "constitution." It's directly above the "u" in "rambunctious," separated by one box. That means that an answer that intersects with both the "t" and, one box down, the "u" has to a) have the letters "t" and "u," and b) have them one letter apart. Can you think of a word that uses both letters, with one between them? Try to write down five here:

1. _____

2. _____

3. _____

4. _____

5. _____

What about "truck" or "tour"? That would work, wouldn't it? A word like "stunt" wouldn't work since the "t" and "u" are right next to each other.

Before you go on, a general instruction. Have you ever seen *The Karate Kid?* No, not the new one with Jackie Chan as the *sensei.* The old one, with Ralph Macchio as the Karate Kid. Well, in that movie, the original *sensei,* played by Pat Morita, tells the Karate Kid this: When it's time to defend yourself, don't use the first move that comes to your mind. Use the *third.*

Why did he say this? Because it forced the Karate Kid not to rely on a single move, but to remember more of the moves the *sensei* had taught him, and—most importantly—because the second or third idea that comes to our minds is often better than the first.

For the same reason, in this exercise, especially as you try to accommodate two letters instead of just one, don't use the first word that comes to your mind. Follow the *sensei,* and choose from at least three.

By the way, do you know what a *sensei* is? If not, you should look it up. A great way to improve your vocabulary is to look up every word that's unfamiliar to you, and then write it down in a special part of your notebook reserved for vocabulary. Do it here for now:

Sensei: _____

WORD 4:

For now, let's stick with "truck." Draw the appropriate boxes on pages B and C, filling in the answer on page C. So, the fourth answer could look like this:

```
                              2
                              D
                              E        4
              1 C O N S T I T U T I O N
                              E        R
                3 R A M B U N C T I O U S
                              M        C
                              I        K
                              N
                              A
                              T
                              I
                              O
                              N
```

Step 2: Can you think of a clue? You could say:

Word 4 (Down): Bigger than a car
or
Word 4 (Down): Comes around to collect garbage

Write the clue on page A.

You should keep going until you have 10 answers/clues down and 10 across. Your three notebook pages should have 20 clues (A), 20 sets of empty, intersecting answer boxes (B), and all the answer boxes filled in (C).

Then, make as many photocopies of sheets A and B as you have members of the family willing to take a stab at the crossword, and watch *them* do the work for a change!

Challenge exercises:

1. Don't use my crossword as a starting point. Begin one from scratch by yourself.

2. Challenge yourself by creating as many answers as you can that intersect with other words more than once. Intersect twice, three times, and four times if you can manage it.

Week 10

Cliché

Purpose: To learn why clichés stunt good writing and to practice avoiding them in your work.

Nothing hurts good writing more than cliché. A cliché is an expression that's been overused to the point that its original meaning has been forgotten.

Here are some examples:
- "early bird catches the worm"
- "drive you up a wall"
- "it takes two to tango"
- "if it ain't broke, don't fix it"

To put it another way, clichés are corny. It isn't that they're wrong; they're not. They were invented, and get used so often, for a reason. But, because they've been used *so* many times, in so many different contexts, they've lost some of their original power. Creative writing depends on originality; you want to say something in a way it has never been said before. Noticing that waves rolling onto a shore are like a tongue spitting out sunflower seeds—that's original and less accurate. Saying that the ocean water is as blue as a teacup is both less original and less accurate. Are teacups necessarily blue? So the comparison isn't effective. But if you have a character telling another with a straight face, "Plenty of other fish in the sea," that's corny and unoriginal. That line has been used so many times, by so many people, in so many different contexts, that it tends to remind us not of the original meaning but of the fact that it's been overused. It's the opposite of specific and precise, and we know that specific and precise are keys to good writing.

Your assignment this week is to sign a pledge to never use clichés in your short stories and poems. You have to come up with 15. Try to come up with at least five from memory. You can find the rest online, or in the newspaper, or on television. Unfortunately, even our news anchors and journalists don't always use their best instincts when communicating.

Once you've come up with your 15, I want you to rewrite the ideas behind them in more original language. The first step is to translate the clichés into ordinary language, to remind ourselves what they actually stand for. For instance, for the four clichés above, that would mean something like:

1. Get there early if you want to be first.
2. You're making me angry.
3. I can't do this by myself.
4. There's nothing wrong here. Leave it alone.

Sometimes, plain, direct language is best. But for the sake of experiment, see if you can phrase the same concepts more originally.

1. You better be on the road by first light. It gets to be a long line by noon.
2. One more comment, and I'm going make it your last.
3. This could stand the help of another body, you know.
4. How about working on something that needs it?

It isn't easy to translate clichés because they're so ingrained in our minds. The process for me was similar to translating abstraction into concreteness. Abstractions can refer to many things; concrete phrasings to only one. So, after reminding myself of the basic meanings buried by the clichés, I tried to imagine specific situations in which one character might want to make the point in question to another.

In the first, I imagined a ranch, a father, a son, perhaps the arrival of some kind of feed or equipment (in limited availability) in a town 40 miles away. In the second, the arguing characters aren't very specific, but the comment itself has more flavor and snap than "You're making me angry." In the third one, again the situation isn't very specific, but the language is unique ("stand the help," "another body"). In the fourth, even though—as in #2 and #3—the characters aren't specific in the finished line of dialogue, they were in my mind as I tried to imagine the situation. I imagined my parents during the weekend, when my father usually heads to his workshop to rearrange his shelves of tools (for the thousandth time!) while my mother harangues him to repaint the laundry room walls (also for the thousandth time).

A question I've often heard is: If the job of poetry and prose is to tell stories about how real people live, and real people use cliché, why is it not acceptable to include cliché in one's writing? It's a fair question. Here are a few answers:

1. First of all, there's a distinction between the author and the people she is writing about. If you can make clear that it's your characters—and not you—who are using the phrase, perhaps it can work. But . . .

2. Do you really want to waste precious room on having characters regurgitate tired phrases? Even the most ordinary people have something unusual and distinguishing about them. Few people are clichés in real life. The gas station attendant may know his Shakespeare and the bank teller may be a whiz in the garden. The job of a writer is to tease this out (unless the whole point is to create a clichéd character). Most people aren't either good or evil, kind or mean, selfish or selfless. They're usually a combination of the two. A writer ought to be much busier figuring out the idiosyncrasies of his characters—what makes them unique, even if they're ordinary—than making them sound like a bunch of other people.

3. Yes, fiction and poetry should describe the lives of ordinary people, but these ordinary people should be people to whom something extraordinary happens, or who discover something extraordinary in themselves, or simply understand something new about life. We're straying into somewhat unrelated territory here: What should stories be about? But it's worth saying a word or two about this. If I had to describe fiction in one sentence, I'd say it's stories about ordinary people who experience extraordinary things. (The word "extraordinary" is used here to mean "other than ordinary" more than "exceptional.") There is nothing extraordinary about cliché, except maybe how extraordinarily unimaginative it is.

The list can go on. Suffice it to say: Down with cliché! Name your 15 below, sign the pledge, and then come up with a way of making each point more originally.

1. _____

2. _____

3. _____

4. _____

5. _____

6. _____

7. _____

8. _____

9. _____

10. _____

11. _____

12. _____

13. _____

14. _____

15. _____

Signature: x _____

Challenge exercise:

Join the "cliché police" for the week of this exercise. Every time you hear or read a cliché, write it down on a piece of paper and "lock it up" in some safe spot. When the week is over, throw the pile of papers out!

Week 11

Concision

Purpose: To understand why concise writing is more powerful than bloated writing and to practice writing concisely.

Concision is the art of saying something in as few words as possible. Why is this an art? Imagine you're listening to someone speak and this person is taking *forever* to make a point that can be made in just a few words. Isn't that annoying? Concise writing makes its point more clearly and powerfully. Compare the following sentences:

• The Giffordses are a pretty nice bunch of people to have on your block. (14 words)

• The Giffordses are marvelous neighbors. (5 words)

Which one sounds sharper, neater, more effective? The second one, I'd argue. Modifiers like "pretty" are usually empty—whatever words they precede will mean "pretty" much the same thing without them. And isn't "bunch of people to have on your block" just a way of saying "neighbors"? There is a famous saying: "This letter would have been shorter if I'd had more time." That is, it takes skill and thought to say something in few words.

This is especially the case in poetry, where the author has only a couple of hundred words to say something, unlike the writer of short stories, who usually has many more. Every word counts! Not one can be wasted! Think of poetry as Facebook, or Twitter, or a text message: you have to make your point in a very limited space.

So, this week, we're going to practice saying things more briefly. Below you'll find 10 sentences. Your job will be to restate them, preserving all the information within them, in as few words as possible. This will be a scored exercise: Each word will count as a point. The fewer points you have at the end of the exercise, the better your score. If your parents, siblings, or friends are willing to compete, you can all go at it as a friendly competition.

Before you start, a couple of other examples:

> "All things considered, it was a decent game for the kids." (11 words)
> "The game went well." (4 words)

Perhaps that "all things considered" hints at some not very good thing that happened during the game, which our condensed version omits, so you may wish to spend some extra words and say something like "*Still*, the game went well" or "*Still*, the game ended well." In this version, we don't know what it was that went wrong—that isn't clear in the original, either—but we do preserve the previous sentence's hint of it through our addition of "still."

If a word isn't absolutely necessary, get rid of it. If the point made by 10 words can be made by three, you should do it. Everyday speech is filled with unnecessary—if not *redundant*—language.

Some of the sentences below use not only unnecessary words, but unnecessary information. For instance, take a sentence like "It was at the Sunday football game that Matt twisted his ankle." What is this sentence trying to tell us? That Matt twisted his ankle at the football game. Does it matter that it took place on Sunday? Not as much.

One more thing: Take a sentence like "I put the key in the ignition and started the car." "Put the key in the ignition" is its own piece of information, but is there a way to start the car without doing that? There isn't, so it's understood and there's no need to mention it in your concise sentence.

A final note: "The game went well" may be shorter than "All things considered, it was a decent game for the kids," but that doesn't make it poetry. Poetry isn't *only* concise, but it's one of the things that poetry has to be. This week, you'll practice simply making the sentence below more concise. In other exercises, you'll practice turning what you come up with into lines of poetry filled with memorable language and vivid description.

Okay, your turn. Relate the next 10 sentences in as few words as possible. Think of each word as a dollar you have to spend! (And by the way, notice that #4 isn't only verbose—the opposite of concise—but full of cliché, too.) You can break up the sentence into two if that helps you be concise. You can flip around the clauses, too. Just preserve the critical pieces of information; the rest is up to you. When you're done, tally up the number of "word dollars" you spent. Compare it to the tally of words in the 10 sentences below.

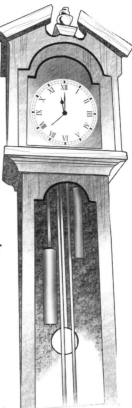

1. Time everlasting clicks away on the clocks all around us.

2. It's one of those things that we'll need a real expert to explain to the folks here.

3. If ever there was a time to get our act together and make some decisions that pertain to this matter, then I'd have to say that time is right about now.

4. All hands on deck! Leave no stone unturned! This doesn't have to be a tough nut to crack.

5. Many times, a sentence can be a whole lot shorter if you just think hard and maybe get rid of a word or two here or there.

6. On any given night, when it's dark and everyone's gone for the day, sometimes what I'll do is go into the control room, flick on the lights, and run around the field all by myself, pretending I'm one of the big football stars.

7. Ladies and gentlemen, the time has come to put away any electronic devices that you may be using at this time.

8. So it goes, my friends, this is the way such things go and no one in this entire world can tell me something other than what I saw here with my own eyes just these last past several days.

9. Under the hot and scalding rays of the warm sun, the leaves and branches and roots of the tree baked in a painful silence.

10. In order to do my homework, I need this book.

Tally of words in the 10 sentences: 240
Your score: _____

Challenge exercise:

Pick 10 sentences randomly from the newspaper and see if you can rewrite them more concisely.

Section 4:
Sound

Weeks 12–17

Week 12

Rhyme

Purpose: To understand the difference between perfect rhymes and near-rhymes and to practice rhyming.

What is **rhyme**?

Rhyme occurs when the final syllable(s) in two words make the same sound—"break" and "take," "spit" and "pit," "sender" and "defender." Say these pairs out loud—do you see what I mean? Exact rhymes like these are called perfect rhymes. The final syllables of perfect rhymes will make the same exact sound, even if they don't use the same letters ("break" and "take"). Only words whose *final* syllables sound the same can be called perfect rhymes, though keep in mind that this may involve more than one concluding syllable, such as in the pair "sender" and "defender" (last *two* syllables make the same sound).

Some word pairs—"passed" and "glass," "composition" and "decision," "towel" and "cower"—have similar final sounds (-tion, -sion) but not exactly the *same* final sounds. These not-exact rhymes are called **near-rhymes.**

So, to review:
Perfect rhyme: Final syllables make same sound
Near-rhyme: Final syllables make similar sound

Part 1: This week, your job will be to come up with 10 words that have two or more syllables and find a perfect rhyme and near-rhyme for each. (Divide your notebook page into three columns and head them "Word," "Perfect Rhyme," and "Near-Rhyme.") So if the word in question is "tractor," a perfect rhyme would be "actor" because the final syllables make the same sound. (Note that in this pair, as in "sender/defender," not only the final syllables make the same sound, but the syllables before them, too.) A near-rhyme for "tractor" could be "batter" or "debtor." (They reproduce the concluding "or" sound but not the "ac" sound before it.)

Write down your list of 10 words here. If you can't think of any, here are some suggestions:

1. hysterical
2. criticize
3. master
4. intervention
5. salamander

Remember that perfect rhymes don't have to be between single words. Salamander rhymes very well with "can't stand her"!

Now, how to find perfect and near-rhymes for all these words? Follow these steps!

1. **Perfect rhyme.** Remember that the final syllable(s) have to match. So, what sounds like "criticize"? How about "eyes" or "despise" or "spies"? These words have very different spellings but they make the same sound, don't they?

2. **Near-rhyme.** A near-rhyme for "criticize" would have a final sound similar to but not exactly like "ize." That means that it could share the "i" sound or the "z" sound but not both. "Sky" and "lie" would both make good near-rhymes (they share the "i" sound); so would "these" and "lose" (they share the "z" sound). You could even get wacky and come up with a word like "design." It has both a "z" sound and an "i" sound but not in its concluding syllable.

Part 2: When you're done, I want you to pick one word/perfect rhyme/near-rhyme trio out of your 10 and write a mini-poem (four lines) that uses all three words. Where you put them is up to you (they don't have to go at the ends of lines) but the four lines need to use them all. Also, you should try your best to make sense instead of composing gibberish. (You might think ahead a little bit and settle only for those kinds of rhymes and near-rhymes for your original word that have something to do with it's meaning or can be made to make sense together in a four-line poem.) So let's see what I can do with "criticize," "penalize" (perfect), and "design" (near):

You criticize without end,
Penalize all my mistakes
As if I made them by design,

A bitter end to this grand plan.
Another try:

> A mean division of our labor:
> I do and you criticize.
> I plead for mercy and you penalize.
> This arrangement needs a new design.

Isn't the second poem more rhythmic to the ear? Either way, placing the rhymes in different places in the four-liners creates different sound effects, even though the words are more or less the same in both poems. The rhyming and near-rhyming words are like echoes, faintly calling to each other from their different places in the poem, making different kinds of music depending on where you've placed them. So think of them as instruments of a kind, lending a poem a special additional sound that stays in the ears a little bit longer than if you had used ordinary words.

Your turn.

Challenge exercise:

Write not one, but *two,* four-liners that use the three rhyme words in different places.

Week 13

Repetition

Purpose: To continue our study of sound effects in poetry through repetition.

Last week, you learned that rhyme creates a certain sound effect in poems. This week, you'll see that repetition does as well. Rhyme is a kind of repetition because it repeats certain syllables. But there are other forms of repetition. You could repeat the same sound over and over throughout a poem, such as by beginning every line of the poem with the letter "t" or by repeating a letter combination like "bl." You could also repeat whole words. You could even repeat whole lines.

To appreciate the power of repetition in poetry, read out loud this poem by Edgar Allan Poe:

"The Bells"

I

Hear the sledges with the bells—
Silver bells!
What a world of merriment their melody foretells!
How they tinkle, tinkle, tinkle,
In the icy air of night!
While the stars that oversprinkle
All the heavens seem to twinkle
With a crystalline delight;
Keeping time, time, time,
In a sort of Runic rhyme,
To the tintinnabulation that so musically wells
From the bells, bells, bells, bells,
Bells, bells, bells—
From the jingling and the tinkling of the bells.

II

Hear the mellow wedding bells—

Golden bells!

What a world of happiness their harmony foretells!

Through the balmy air of night

How they ring out their delight!

From the molten-golden notes,

And all in tune,

What a liquid ditty floats

To the turtle-dove that listens, while she gloats

On the moon!

Oh, from out the sounding cells

What a gush of euphony voluminously wells!

How it swells!

How it dwells

On the Future!—how it tells

Of the rapture that impels

To the swinging and the ringing

Of the bells, bells, bells,

Of the bells, bells, bells, bells,

Bells, bells, bells—

To the rhyming and the chiming of the bells!

III

Hear the loud alarum bells—

Brazen bells!

What a tale of terror, now, their turbulency tells!

In the startled ear of night

How they scream out their affright!

Too much horrified to speak,

They can only shriek, shriek,

Out of tune,

In a clamorous appealing to the mercy of the fire,

In a mad expostulation with the deaf and frantic fire,

Leaping higher, higher, higher,

With a desperate desire,

And a resolute endeavor

Now—now to sit or never,

By the side of the pale-faced moon.

Oh, the bells, bells, bells!

What a tale their terror tells
Of despair!
How they clang, and clash, and roar!
What a horror they outpour
On the bosom of the palpitating air!
Yet the ear it fully knows,
By the twanging
And the clanging,
How the danger ebbs and flows;
Yet the ear distinctly tells,
In the jangling
And the wrangling,
How the danger sinks and swells,
By the sinking or the swelling in the anger of the bells—
Of the bells,
Of the bells, bells, bells, bells,
Bells, bells, bells—
In the clamor and the clangor of the bells!

IV
Hear the tolling of the bells—
Iron bells!
What a world of solemn thought their monody compels!
In the silence of the night,
How we shiver with affright
At the melancholy menace of their tone!
For every sound that floats
From the rust within their throats
Is a groan.
And the people—ah, the people—
They that dwell up in the steeple,
All alone,
And who tolling, tolling, tolling,
In that muffled monotone,
Feel a glory in so rolling
On the human heart a stone—
They are neither man nor woman—

They are neither brute nor human—
They are Ghouls:

And their king it is who tolls;
And he rolls, rolls, rolls,
Rolls
A paean from the bells!
And his merry bosom swells
With the paean of the bells!
And he dances, and he yells;
Keeping time, time, time,
In a sort of Runic rhyme,
To the paean of the bells,
Of the bells—
Keeping time, time, time,
In a sort of Runic rhyme,
To the throbbing of the bells,
Of the bells, bells, bells—
To the sobbing of the bells;
Keeping time, time, time,
As he knells, knells, knells,
In a happy Runic rhyme,
To the rolling of the bells,
Of the bells, bells, bells—
To the tolling of the bells,
Of the bells, bells, bells, bells,
Bells, bells, bells—
To the moaning and the groaning of the bells.[10]

Quick: What word is ringing like mad through your head right now? I bet it's "bells"! Doesn't this poem read differently than if the word "bells" appeared only once? Repetition doesn't necessarily make for *better* poetry, and there's no rule saying you have to use it. It just makes for a different kind of poetry, a sound unlike what you get without it—interesting because poetry is devoted to exploring not only meaning, but sound.

Your turn. This week, you're going to take one of the poems you've written so far this year and change it by repeating the same word in it at least 10 times while still making sense. What that word is depends on what your poem is about. You should definitely pick something that will make it easier for your poem to make sense.

---

10. From "The Bells," by Edgar Allan Poe (Philadelphia, 1881).

Optional: Instead of squeezing repetition into a poem that was written with another goal in mind, you may find it easier to write a brand-new, 20-line poem that uses the same word at least 10 times and still makes sense.

It might look something like this:

> I dream a dream of many wishes
> A dream of candy, pizza, knishes
> A dream of summer, sand, and sea
> A dream of you, a dream of me.
>
> A dream is like an empty road
> That takes the dreamer where he goes
> The dream-road has no other cars,
> Only the road and dreamy stars.

You'll notice a couple of things: First of all, I found myself rhyming the first and second lines, and the third and fourth lines, in each stanza. Secondly, I utilized a near-rhyme in lines 1 and 2 of the second stanza ("road," "goes"). Also, I made my life a little easier by modifying the selected word ("dream"): "dreamer," "dream-road," "dreamy." All of this is acceptable.

What makes this exercise interesting is that you're practicing repetition while trying to make sense, a more advanced version of the challenge you encountered in your alphabet poem exercise: figuring out how to make sense while satisfying a restriction in what you can say.

Repetition in poetry resembles choruses in music: a memorable hook. I bet your head will be ringing for hours, if not days, with the word you choose to repeat 10 times, just like a song chorus that "gets stuck in your head." It's no accident it gets stuck in your head—that's the point of a chorus: it repeats and repeats.

Challenge exercises:

1. Instead of repeating a word, repeat a sound. The sound could be a single letter, like "t," but because "t" appears in so many words as it is, you'll want to highlight it more by, say, having every line of the poem start with a letter beginning with "t."

2. Instead of repeating a single letter, repeat a sound, like "bl," in as many words as possible throughout the poem (and at least once a line).

Week 14

Assonance, consonance, alliteration

Purpose: To learn about other sound effects in poetry.

This week, we're going to focus on other kinds of rhyme: when syllables *inside* words, rather than at the end of them, make the same sound. We're also going to learn about repeating sounds at the very beginning of words.

If you remember, in perfect rhyme, the *final* syllables of two words make the same sound ("coast" and "boast," "tree" and "me," "treasure" and "measure"). In "inner" rhyme, non-final syllables make the same sound. Take, for instance, "Mike" and "brine." They don't have perfect rhyme, but the "i" sound in "Mike" and the "i" sound in "brine" are the same. Take a word like "criticize." You could inner-rhyme the first sound ("crit") with "sit," "mitt," "critter," or "bitter," and the third sound ("ci") with "sky" or "lie."

Inner-rhyme using vowels is called **assonance** ("coast" and "moat," "coast" and "low"). Inner-rhyme using consonants is called **consonance** ("bench" and "sentry"; there's assonance here, too, between the e's). Remember: the letters don't have to be identical; only the sounds made by them need be. The e's in "bench" and "sentry" have assonance; the a's in "sparrow" and "car" do not. Let's look at some examples in published poems. Refer back to Edgar Allan Poe's "The Bells" from last week's exercise on repetition. Take the first line:

> "Hear the sledges with the bells—"

Do we see any assonance or consonance here? "Sledges" and "bells" supplies us with examples of both consonance in the l's and assonance in the e's). Read the line out loud; do the similar sounds stand out to you?

How about the first line of the second section:

> "Hear the mellow wedding bells…"

Can you figure out where the consonance and assonance are here? (Hint:

The answer is pretty similar to the first example. The sounds not only echo each other but also the first line of the preceding section.) The assonance in this line is even more pronounced than in the earlier example, because there are three examples of it. Read the line out loud. Do you hear the rhythm produced by that same sound repeating over and over?

Now look at "Fire and Ice," a poem by Robert Frost:

> Some say the world will end in fire,
> Some say in ice.
> From what I've tasted of desire
> I hold with those who favor fire.
> But if it had to perish twice,
> I think I know enough of hate
> To say that for destruction ice
> Is also great
> And would suffice.[11]

Jot down some examples of assonance or consonance. Then compare with some I found:

Consonance:
- "**s**ome" and "**s**ay" (1ˢᵗ and 2ⁿᵈ line)
- "**w**orld and **w**ill" (1ˢᵗ line)
- "thi**nk**" and "**kn**ow" (6ᵗʰ line)

Assonance:
- "I h**o**ld with th**o**se who favor fire" (4ᵗʰ line; recall that assonance refers to similar *sounds*, not simply identical letters. The "o" in "who" makes a completely different sound (oo) than the "o"s in "hold" and "those" (oh). So does the "o" in "favor," which makes more of an "e" sound.)
- "**I** think **I** know" (6ᵗʰ line)

Whenever the repeating sounds occur in the *first* letters of the word, that's called **alliteration**. So "some" and "say," and "world" and "will," are examples of both **consonance** and **alliteration**. "Some," "say," and "ice" are an example of consonance but not alliteration because it isn't the first letters that match in all three. Same for "think" and "know."

---

11. From *American Poetry, 1922: A Miscellany* (New York, 1922), p. 25.

Let's quickly review:

- Assonance happens when vowel sounds are repeated.
- Consonance happens when consonant sounds are repeated.
- Alliteration happens when repeated sounds come at the beginnings of words.

Now, it's time to practice. Do the 10 exercises below. For all of them, prepositions (of, to) and articles (a, the) don't count toward the total number of words or the assigned sound scheme.

1. Write a sentence that provides at least three examples of **assonance**. (You can start by repeating simple sounds like those of a single letter, for instance, "**Pat Sam** the c**a**t.")

2. Do the same for **consonance**.

3. Write a minimum five-word sentence where each word begins with the same letter (d). [**alliteration**]

4. Write a minimum five-word sentence where each word begins with the same letter (letter up to you). [**alliteration**]

5. Write a minimum five-word sentence where each word begins with the letter "b" or "v." [**Near-alliteration**]

6. Write a sentence that provides at least three examples of **assonance**. Try to repeat a sound made by more than one letter, and try to use different letters in at least two of the sounds. Example: The gr**ow**n d**oe** tramples the b**ou**gh.

7. Write a sentence that provides at least three examples of **consonance**, but not alliteration. Example: The bra**ts** a**te** all the da**tes**.

8. Find an example of each of this week's three sound devices in published text, be it a newspaper, a magazine, an instruction manual, or a religious text. With alliteration, even just two consecutive words beginning with the same sound qualify.

The point of this exercise isn't to get you to twist into a verbal pretzel. Neither is it to get you to memorize the proper names for all these devices. It's to get you to listen to the different sounds created by these devices, just as in music.

To finish up this week, please recite your sentences, then have a friend or your mentor read them out loud. As you listen, try not to listen for their meaning. Close your eyes—not when you're the one reading, obviously!—and focus on the sound.

Challenge exercises:

1. Go back to all the poems you've written this year and underline examples of assonance, consonance, and alliteration.

2. Go to your favorite poem (if you don't have one, find one online; if you can't think of one, how about "The Rime of the Ancient Mariner" by Samuel Taylor Coleridge) and underline every example of assonance, consonance, and alliteration. Remember that it's the sound that has to match, not only (or necessarily) the letters. So, the "a"s in "ancient" and "mariner" actually don't have assonance, as they're pronounced differently.

Week 15

Sound vs. meaning
(Eavesdropping, Part II)

Purpose: To learn about how sound works in poetry.

Do you remember your eavesdropping exercise from the fiction section? You collected 20 lines of dialogue from the people you listened to that week. This week, you're going to take those 20 lines and arrange them into several 20-line poems.

Step One

For the first one, you should do nothing to the snippets of dialogue you collected. You already have them written down in order in your notebook: Just re-write them in exactly that order. (If some of the snippets include more than one sentence, pick a single sentence from the snippet.) Voila! That's your first poem. Read it out loud.

A word about reading poetry out loud: It's not complicated, but there *is* some art to it. For instance, it's customary to pause for the slightest moment at the end of each line of a poem. This may sound odd because far from all poetry lines end with a period. But that's the point—you pause anyway. You should also pause when you run into a period—no matter where you find it—and semi-pause when you run into a comma. Lots of pausing, right?

Step Two

For your second poem, try to organize these 20 random lines into a poem that makes as much sense as possible. Don't worry if you have a hard time getting the poem to make sense—it's almost impossible to. I just want you to play around with the lines to see what you can come up with.

When you organize your poem, break the 20 lines into *at least* four stanzas. (Stanzas, you'll remember, are groups of lines in a poem. They're separated by a blank line.) You could have five stanzas of four lines apiece, four stanzas of five lines apiece, six (or however many) stanzas of differing numbers of lines...

How should you decide where the stanzas break?

For some poets, each stanza is about something new in the poem: a new idea, the next action in the situation the poem describes. For others, it isn't so exact; they'll run the same idea or action across different stanzas to create an effect, beginning a new stanza in the middle of a sentence. There's no science to it. Just arrange the stanzas so that you like the way the final poem sounds. We'll talk more about stanzas in the next level of this series.

Read this poem out loud as well. Pause not only at the end of each line but at the end of each stanza.

Challenge exercises:

1. Do Poem #2 over. (You'll be surprised by how much better this second version will be.)

2. Poem #3: Collect 20 new lines of dialogue from around you, but with the foreknowledge that you will have to use them to write a 20-line poem that has to make as much sense as possible. Therefore, you should be listening for lines that might "go together" well.

3. Poem #4: After you've done the exercise for Week 18, which directs you to write a poem from scratch without any restrictions imposed by me, come back to this exercise and read your poems back to back, in order from most random (#1) to least random (#4).

I wanted you to do this exercise to get you used to the idea that poetry is about more than meaning. This is another of its key differences from fiction. Poems aren't completely random (though some poets are harder to understand than others), but poetry relies on meaning much less than fiction does. In poetry, we listen to how different words and lines sound next to each other as much as to understand some larger meaning. In this sense, poetry is more "musical" than fiction. Your first poem is an example of what I'm talking about, with each new poem in the four-poem series this lesson references making a little more sense.

Week 16

A poetic ransom note

Purpose: To understand that poetry is about more than meaning.

Last week, you made a poem out of a random collection of lines. This week, your job is to make a poem out of a random collection of letters.

Ever seen a movie where a ransom note is put together using words, letters, and phrases cut from a newspaper or magazine? That's what you're going to do this week, except you won't be ransoming anyone, and you'll be trying to make a poem out of your cuttings.

Start by finding 10 printed items that you can cut up: Newspaper, magazine, instruction manual, cereal box, etc. From **each one**, cut out 10 individual words, so that you end up with 100 words. (If you'd like a word, but it comes from a printed item that you shouldn't cut up—like a book or warranty—feel free to write it yourself on a piece of paper.) Try your best to cut out these 10 words from 10 different places in the newspaper or manual or what have you. Don't think too hard about what you cut out, except to get a healthy variety of short words and long ones; verbs, nouns, and adjectives; as well as **articles** (a, the), **prepositions** (of, to, etc.), commas, and periods. (Your commas and periods don't count toward the totals. Get a handful of each. It's also okay to draw your own comma or period by hand, if you like.)

Now, try to arrange your 100 words into a poem with as many or as few lines as you'd like. These lines can be arranged in a single unbroken stanza or broken up into several, each with the same—or not the same—number of lines.

The whole idea is to put surprising strings of words together: "the plummeting bulldozer," "sky with the ache" ("ache along with the sky" can be fun if you have a word like "along" or "with"). The poem doesn't have to make perfect sense, but it should be grammatically correct ("sky ache the with" doesn't work).

You should also feel free to cut out images. These won't count toward your totals, but may be fun to include. You might have a bowl of flakes, or a row of military tanks, and might think to include them in unexpected places. A bowl of flakes might accompany a sentence that mentions the word politics. The tank photo might go next to a sentence that mentions a fish. (Get it?) It's a way to play with the different meanings of the same word. But it doesn't even have to be that clever. It might simply be funny or interesting to have a picture of rain next to your sentence about the aching sky. (How do you know the sky is aching? It's raining.)

You may need posterboard on which to fit all of your words. Paste them on with glue or tape. And have fun!

Challenge exercises:

1. Purchase a set of magnetic poetry for the fridge. Write a 5-stanza, 20-line poem using the fridge magnet words.

2. Have your mentor or a friend choose the 100 words to cut out, and write a poem using *those*.

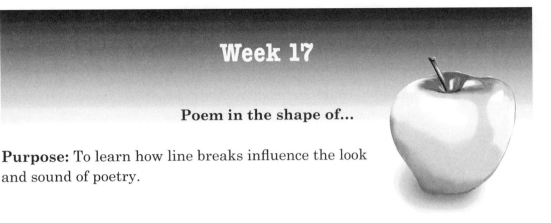

Week 17

Poem in the shape of...

Purpose: To learn how line breaks influence the look and sound of poetry.

Take a poem, any poem. It could be a poem that you've written this year, or it could be a published poem that you love. Either way, read the poem carefully several times, so you're very familiar with it. Your job this week will be to present the poem in five different shapes. (If the poem is long, you can pick a portion of it, perhaps several stanzas.) That is, you're not writing anything new—hooray, right?—only shaping. So, for instance, if you wanted to present your poem in the shape of an apple, it might look something like this:

poem

poem

poem

poem

poem poem

poem poem poem

poem poem poem poem

poem poem poem poem poem

poem poem poem poem poem poem

poem poem poem poem poem

poem poem poem poem

poem poem poem

poem poem

Here's an example using actual words: a poem about a tree in the shape of a tree:

Do you
think it is easy
to stand upright all day?
To bend with every wind, and
lose hair every autumn? Change
colors like a chameleon? Without an
umbrella to keep dry from the sky?
Enough, I am ready to say. But
then I remember Newton.
And John Muir. And
van Gogh.
They
make
this
long
life
worth
living.

Here's the same poem in the shape of a pyramid:

Do
you think it is
easy to stand upright
all day? To bend with every
wind, and lose hair every autumn?
Change colors like a chameleon? Without
an umbrella to keep dry from the sky? Enough,
I am ready to say. But then I remember Newton. And
John Muir. And van Gogh. They make this long life worth living.

Read these poems out loud, taking care to pause slightly at the end of each line. Do they sound different to you? Can you say how? Surely you have noticed that poetry differs from prose in that its lines don't end at the right margin of the page. For poets, this is a wonderful opportunity to influence the sound of the poem. In deciding where to end their lines, they can create very different-sounding poems.

For instance, in the first version of the tree poem above—the one that looks like a tree—the poem starts off as quickly as the pyramid version. The lines are short: "Do you/think it is easy..." The lines briefly grow longer, but then shorten again, before racing to the end with extra-short lines that feature no more than a single word. If you're taking care to pause properly at the end of each line (whether reading out loud or under your breath), the poem creates a particular rhythm: quick, slow, quick, very quick.

The pyramid poem is different: It goes from very quick to very slow with each line longer than the last, creating a very different feeling from the tree shape—quick, slow, very slow, verrrrry slow.

Why do poets consider line breaks such a useful tool? It's because the sound of the poem can be used to echo what the poem is about. Let's say your poem is about a woodchuck tapping away at a tree. Tat-tat-tat. Tat-tat-tat. It's a rapid-fire sound. So if you had very long, slow lines, that wouldn't be a good match, would it? But what if your poem was about a balloon floating gently through the sky? Longer, slower lines might be just what you need.

Line breaks are wonderful tools for another reason: The end of a line presents the poet with an opportunity for a little bit of suspense. Look at the line, in the pyramid version above, that ends "like a..." "Like a" what, you wonder. Your eyes race to the next line to find out the answer. Line breaks are a way for poets to give the reader a little kick in the pants, to make them curious to keep going.

This is why I would like you to write up the same poem in five different shapes—so you can see how differently the same poem sounds depending on where you break up the lines.

Note that I never broke up a word into syllables to make it fit a line. Only complete words will do, and if you have a tricky narrow space like the stem of an apple, fill each line with no less than an entire single word. (It's okay, by the way, if your last line doesn't reach the end of the shape. The goal here is to give you a general idea, not twist you into an engineering pretzel.) One more thing: Do you know who Isaac Newton was? John Muir? Vincent van Gogh? (And what they have to do with trees?) Unfamiliar names work the same way as unfamiliar words; if you don't recognize them, look them up. They're very likely to have Wikipedia entries, which make for great starting points.

You may do this exercise by hand or on the computer. If you're stuck for a poem, how about the first section of Edgar Allan Poe's "The Bells?" from the lesson on repetition?

I

Hear the sledges with the bells—
Silver bells!
What a world of merriment their melody foretells!
How they tinkle, tinkle, tinkle,
In the icy air of night!
While the stars that oversprinkle
All the heavens seem to twinkle
With a crystalline delight;
Keeping time, time, time,
In a sort of Runic rhyme,
To the tintinnabulation that so musically wells
From the bells, bells, bells, bells,
Bells, bells, bells—
From the jingling and the tinkling of the bells.

So, for instance, this poem in the shape of a tree might look something like this:

Hear
the sledges
with the bells—Silver
bells! What a world of merriment
their melody foretells! How they tinkle,
tinkle, tinkle, In the icy air of night! While the
stars that oversprinkle All the heavens
seem to twinkle With a crystalline
delight; Keeping time, time,
time, In a sort of Runic
rhyme, To the
tintinnabulation
that so musically
wells From the
bells, bells, bells,
bells, Bells, bells,
bells—From the
jingling and the
tinkling of the bells.

If you're stumped, here are some ideas for shapes in which you could rewrite your poem.

1. Mountain
2. Fence
3. Car
4. Fish
5. Blender
6. Snake

When you're finished, read the original and then the five poems in each poem-shape out loud, taking care to pause at the end of each line. Do the poems sound different to you? Can you put words to how?

Challenge exercise:

Instead of using a poem you've already written or a published poem, write a new poem for this exercise.

Section 5:
Write a Poem from Scratch

Week 18

Week 18

Time to write a poem

Purpose: To write a poem from scratch, using all that you've learned this year, but with no restrictions coming from me.

We'll close out the poetry portion of our first year together by having you write a poem from scratch. This week is when you bring together all the skills you've learned so far: description, rhyme, line breaks, comparisons, concision. It may help you to quickly review the lessons for this year before you get started, to refresh your memory.

You don't have to use them all, but when you do, please take care to utilize the things you learned this semester. Avoid clichés. Think about where your lines end. Use sound devices to your advantage. And so on.

What should your poem be about? This is completely up to you. Even the length is up to you, though don't cheat by writing a really short poem only because you want to get this assignment over with quickly. Aim for at least 20 lines, as we have throughout the course.

I'll give you two ideas to get you started, though feel free to choose one of your own.

One of the things we haven't discussed about poetry is how freeing it is. This is true for short stories, also. You don't *have to* write a poem from your own perspective. You could write it from the perspective of a seal, a convict locked up in Alcatraz, or a sailor in the 1700s. You could write it from the perspective of your mom, or your dog, or your grocer. Poetry is a license to leave your body and go skulking around in the lives of others. It's fun, but work, too. A sailor in the 1700s will probably see life very differently from you today, which requires you to spend some time thinking about what life must have been like for him. At the same time, he's still a human being—he sleeps, eats, maybe misses his family—so he'll share a lot with you, too. (Though he probably eats very different food and sleeps on a very different kind of mattress than you do. You might want to imagine what kind exactly.) In the end, you could even write a poem about your relationship to this unknown person. Your only limit is your imagination.

You can take an extra leap and write your poem from the perspective of someone you don't like or understand, or something that scares you. It's a great way of making whatever it is less scary and confusing. Once we get into the mind of someone and imagine his or her life, more often than not that person will stop being so scary because we understand a little bit better what makes him/her tick.

The other idea has to do with your lesson from two weeks ago. Remember all those concise sentences you created out of those baggy ones I made up? You might remember a point I made: Conciseness alone doesn't make good poetry. "Things went well" may be concise, but not very interesting or memorable as a line of poetry. ("Things" is pretty generic; "went well" is ordinary language for around the dinner table, not the charged language poems should have.) So what you can do this week is a) arrange your 10 concise sentences into a poetic order (kind of like your Eavesdropping II exercise) and b) rewrite them, keeping them as concise as you can, to make them more interesting. In short, turn those 10 random sentences into a coherent, memorable poem.

There are plenty of other ideas out there. Write a poem about what a bird sees flying over your town, or a poem called "I used to be but now I am," or a poem where each line starts with a number, from 20 to one, in the style of "12 Days of Christmas." Make your poem about anything you like. You've worked hard this semester, and you've earned the right to write about whatever you want!

Before you close this book for the year, remember to revisit Challenge Exercise #3 for Week 15!

Mentor Materials

for

Part II: POETRY

Mentor Materials

Section 1: Introduction to Poetry
(or, I'm a poet and I don't know it)
Weeks 1–2

Week 1—The alphabet exercise

Purpose: To begin to understand the difference between fiction and poetry.

Here's an example of one complete alphabet poem, using the starting lines above and utilizing both complete sentences and fragments, and both complete and incomplete clauses:

A screeching noise woke me up.
Before I got up, I looked at the alarm clock.
Crazy, I thought: It's not even 5:00 a.m.
Downstairs, everything was quiet.
Everyone still seemed to be sleeping.
Funny things happen in the night while everyone sleeps.
Go back upstairs, I told myself; drink some
Hot milk to help fall asleep.
It's only 5:00, after all!
Just as I returned upstairs,
Ka-boom! I heard again from downstairs.
Looks like I'm not getting very
Much sleep to-
Night, I thought.
Or maybe I should just ignore the noise?
Put the pillow over my head, make it
Quiet with earplugs, and finally get some
Rest?
Sounds
Totally
Unlikely!
Very unlikely.
What do you have to do to catch
Yourself some
Zzzzzzzzzzzs around here?

To create this alphabet poem, I thought ahead only as far as the next letter. (In fact, I covered up every letter but the next one, which made the task more manageable.) Working on, for instance, "s," I was, in the back of my mind, thinking ahead to "t" and trying to think of words that begin with "t" that could go together in a phrase with something that begins with "s" (it's not always possible but it was, in this case).

Another way to drum up ideas is to come up in advance with a list of words that begin with the necessary alphabet letter and also have to do with sleep. (Quiet, pillow, noise, earplugs.) In fact, you may wish to have the writer come up with 25 Words That Have To Do With Sleep (if she's writing an alphabet poem about being woken up in the middle of the night) before even starting the exercise. That will give her a whole bunch of words to work with and around as she constructs the poem.

Another way to help the writer if she's stuck on a particular letter is to get her to open a pocket dictionary and flip through the letter until a light-bulb goes off and she finds something with which she'd like to work. (Another option is to simply write out 20, say, "p" words from the dictionary and try to make one work.)

You might ask how the poem above is different from a piece of prose chopped up into 20 lines. It's a fair question—there *isn't* much difference right now. My example is not exhibiting any of the things that distinguish poetry from prose except for line breaks—there is no rhyme scheme, no meter, and—most importantly but least quantifiably—the language is slack and colloquial, and the imagery basic. Don't mistake this for poetry: it merely mimics the writer's stage of development. As we proceed through this course and on to further levels of this series, our poetry will improve in tandem.

Week 2—Acronym poem

Purpose: Write a poem where each new line begins not with the next letter of the alphabet but with the next letter of an acronym (ASAP, TTYL, CIA).

If the writer is stuck, help him the same way you did in Week 1: Take a break from the assignment and brainstorm words that begin with the necessary letter. Or flip through the dictionary—a great way to expand vocabulary! Here are some other acronyms you could recommend in case the writer is having trouble coming up with the five he needs to choose on his own. You can either give the writer the acronym and ask him to guess what it stands for, or give the writer the words/phrase and ask him to come up with the acronym:

AAMOF (as a matter of fact)
CEO (chief executive officer)
IKWUM (I know what you mean)
JTLYK (just to let you know)
POAHF (put on a happy face)
NIMBY (not in my backyard)
POTUS (President of the United States)
WHO (World Health Organization)

You'll notice that acronyms often correspond to clichés; it's precisely because the phrase is used so often that someone developed an acronym. We'll have a lesson on the problem with cliché later in the course; for now, it's great that the writer will be steering the acronym away from the cliché, endowing those over-familiar letters with new meaning.

As you probably noticed, this lesson uses the challenge exercises to gradually ramp up the restrictions under which the writer has to produce a poem that still makes sense. This is one week where I would strongly advise taking extra time to do all the challenge exercises, as they have this sequential nature.

Mentor Materials

Section 2: Description
Weeks 3–6

<u>**Week 3**—As unhappy as a bluefish at the end of a fishing line:</u> **Comparisons**

Purpose: To learn how to use similes and metaphors.

Because metaphors are difficult to prompt (see #10, for instance), make sure the writer answers with an actual comparison. But this comparison need not be literal. That is, the writer could compare the star-studded sky to a face studded with freckles, or she could compare the star-studded sky to a necklace. As long as both images share the *dominant* detail—many small dots in the same place—it works. But it's critical that the writer focuses on the detail declared dominant by the assignment. That is, #10 asks the writer to compare the studdedness of the sky—not the color of the sky, and not anything else related to astronomy. Here are some answers that could work for #10:

> The stars studded the sky, a freckled dark mask.
> The stars studded the sky, a holey undershirt.
> The stars studded the sky, a necklace of pearls.
> The stars studded the sky, a box of nails holding up a dark curtain.

In #4, the dominant detail is the greenness of the apple.

In #5 (less obvious), it's the smallness and fragility of the yacht in the "vast blue sea," so the writer would have to come up with a comparison that stresses this, for instance "nothing more than a sapling in a windstorm."

In #6, the writer would have to compare Meredith to someone fast, someone light, someone casting the troubles off his shoulders—a puma? an Olympic torchbearer? one of those messengers sprinting from town to town in the Greek myths?

In #7, the dominant detail is left up to the writer. For me, threading a needle is like "trying to get my cat into his carrier" (dominant detail: generic difficulty) or "like trying to hike through a slot canyon in New Mexico" (dominant detail: physical narrowness), but I can just as easily imagine an answer such as "Threading a needle is like administering a shot" (dominant detail: the act of poking a thin item into/through something else) or "like sinking a jump shot" (generically putting one thing into another).

In #8: Clearly, "he" was an optimist. But the writer can't say that; she has to come up with a metaphor whose dominant detail is optimism: "He bought lottery tickets every day." Or, "He would have been the one cheerful guy on the *Titanic*."

In #9: The dominant detail here seems to be pretty well-defined: The notion of stealth, an object moving through a concealing space, like a submarine, a special-forces soldier, or a thief.

Week 4—Abstract into concrete

Purpose: To come up with concrete words for abstract objects and ideas.

The distinction between concrete and abstract is, well, quite abstract to young writers. But it's a critical one for good writing. Reading is more difficult than watching television—the reader has to form images based on the words by himself. That work is hard. The writer has to help the reader by making it as easy as possible to imagine what he is saying—not by using simple words or images, but by being as concrete as possible. Think about it: If my novel says "Sam loved Arianna," you get the gist of his feelings about her but little more. *How* does he love her? If I tell you about him observing her with a slightly fearful wonder as she swings with their daughter in a park, wouldn't that tell you more?

Don't worry if the writer doesn't quite grasp the distinction between concrete and abstract at this point. The more important thing is to get him to practice specificity, vividness, and concreteness. If he becomes stuck in coming up with a list of five abstractions, help him by performing the chocolate-sauce test. Can you pour chocolate sauce on generosity? On fear? On politics?

If the writer is confused about what kinds of concrete images he ought to come up with for his abstract terms, ask: What does it make you think of? Take a break from the exercise and jot down five associated images for each one. Chances are the writer will produce concrete images in response. It's our natural storytelling impulse to translate from abstract into concrete, even when we aren't working on exercises or writing poems. The images the writer produces can feed his poem for this week's exercise.

Week 5—Colors into words

Purpose: To compose a poem of concrete images about an abstract painting.

This week's exercise expands on the skills taught last week, but on a higher level: the writer has to write a full poem, focusing on a single object. If the writer is stuck, prompt her by asking her to write down 10 things that she notices about the painting. Ask:

> What are the colors?
> Are the colors solid or mixed with others?
> What are the shapes?
> Are they equal?
> How are they divided?
> What other things (in the "real world") are black, grey, and/or grey-mixed-with-white? Where else in the world do we find two rectangles? A straight line?
> How would you feel if you encountered this painting in the basement on a rainy day? At church? In the supermarket?

Like last week, have the writer use the answers to these questions as starting points toward concrete images that will fill a poem. The poem can consist of many unrelated images and feelings (see Challenge Exercise #1), but you can challenge the writer to make the poem more coherent than that by focusing on one or several things. For instance, the whole poem can be all about the memory of the painting in the writer's mind throughout the day, and the surprising moments that she thought about it. Something like:

> In the morning, it is the color of Mom's coffee on an overcast day.
> By the afternoon, it's our vegetable garden, rich with black earth.
> By nighttime, it's the dark night itself, the lights going out one by one, the dreams awaiting their turn.

Other options: The writer can write a narrative poem in which she describes a visit to the museum to view the painting, or a heist of the painting from the museum by thieves (and what *they* think of it). She can write a comparison poem, trying to understand the painting through other objects that have the same colors. She can even write it as Mark Rothko, musing on what it's like to have all those people out there constantly guessing what his painting could "mean."

Week 6—Going where no man has gone before

Purpose: To use our imagination to envision invisible things.

The writer has been given very specific guidance in the lesson, so you should not need to add to it. You can help the writer by prompting him, using the questions mentioned in the lesson; sometimes it is helpful for writers to answer questions orally before putting their thoughts into writing.

Mentor Materials

Section 3: Getting the words right
Weeks 7–11

Week 7—Synonyms, antonyms, homonyms

Purpose: To learn how to use synonyms, antonyms, and homonyms.

Here is a list of potential answers for 1a:

1. Shiny
2. Irritating
3. Tasty
4. Whine
5. Petition

If the writer is stuck, prompt her by asking: Of which words does "bright" remind you? She might give you associations rather than synonyms—sun, sky, maybe a piece of clothing. If she hasn't thrown out an adjective, ask her if "bright" reminds her of any. Find an item that could be said to be bright or—here's the synonym—shiny, and ask her to describe it.

There are more and less precise synonyms and antonyms. And so, while our goal here isn't necessarily to force the writer to come up with the most exact equivalent or contrast, if she volunteers something like "disgusting" as an antonym for "delicious," ask her if "disgusting" must necessarily refer to food. She'll probably realize that it doesn't, and, as such, is a bit broad. Must "tasteless" or "stale" refer to food? Those aren't catch-alls for all the ways in which food can be undelicious (which isn't really a word), but at least they definitely have to do with taste. ("Bland" is another one.)

A sample list of answers for 1b:
1. Ignite
2. Mobility
3. Fix
4. Stoic
5. Bland

A sample list of answers for 1c:

1. I'll, isle
2. Idle, idyll
3. By, bye
4. Holey, wholly
5. Rowed, rode

A variety of online sites such as the one below can help you familiarize yourself with homonyms. Consult them together with the writer.

http://www.cooper.com/alan/homonym_list.html

You may need to introduce the writer to a thesaurus. If you're not familiar with thesaurus use yourself, see Appendix 1.

Week 8—If I could count the ways

Purpose: To practice making the same point in many different ways.

Here are a couple of sentences the writer might use if he is having trouble coming up with his own:

1. The store was closed, so I had to drive another 40 miles for vegetables. (Key general concepts: store, motion, food)
2. The players couldn't score and the fans didn't cheer, but the team didn't lose. (Key general concepts: Players, audience, outcome.)

And here are some strategies for seeing the sentence in a new light, to make rewriting it easier:

1. Break up the sentence into more than one sentence. (The store was closed. I had to drive another 40 miles. I needed vegetables.)
2. Flip around the clauses, putting the third one first, the first one second, etc. (I needed vegetables and had to drive 40 miles because the store was closed.)
3. Make three sentences consisting of nothing more than single words (synonyms for the key concepts in the sentence), as in #7 in the writer text. (Food. Closed. Drive.)

Week 9—Crossword

Purpose: To look very, very closely at the letters that make up various words.

I provided Words 1–4; if the writer is stuck in coming up with #5, ask her to pick a letter combination in the answers that have already been inserted into the crossword. What about the "m" in "rambunctious" and the "c" in "truck"? They're three boxes away from each other. The writer could open the dictionary and try to find words that start with "m" and have "c" in the fifth spot (Morocco, menace). Words that don't *start* with "m," but where the "c" follows the "m" three boxes later, are fine, too, though those are tougher to find.

Another option for Word 5 is the "e" in "determination" and the "r" in "truck"—same number of boxes away from each other. What about "enterprise" or "Eeyore"?

Of course, it's fine to use words that intersect with others in only one spot. The "c" in "chore" intersects nicely with the "c" in "constitution." So does the "c" in "Massachusetts."

(If the writer chooses to start a new crossword from scratch, follow the logic provided in the lesson for Words 1-4.)

If, after the writer has finished, you have trouble with one of the crossword entries, prompt her for an alternate clue. Or ask her to use the Five Senses to provide more information about the answer. If the answer isn't concrete—say, determination—ask her to translate it into a concrete image, as she learned in Weeks 4 and 5. Either that, or it's time for charades!

Week 10—Cliché

Purpose: To learn why clichés stunt good writing and to practice avoiding them in your work.

Here are some more examples of cliché that might—should!—appear in the writer's list:

- "laughter is the best medicine"
- "the more things change, the more they stay the same"

- "pot calling the kettle black"
- "old meets new"
- "rags to riches"
- "between a rock and a hard place"
- "it was a dark and stormy night"
- "let sleeping dogs lie"
- "15 minutes of fame"
- "reign supreme"
- "a good time was had by all"
- "actions speak louder than words"
- "two wrongs don't make a right"
- "down to earth"

You might also consult these sites:

http://suspense.net/whitefish/cliche.htm
http://suspense.net/whitefish/cliche.htm#all_talk,_no_action)

Point out use of cliché to the writer every time you encounter it in the course of the week. As the challenge exercise suggests, make a game out of it, in which he joins the cliché police for the week (maybe a badge?) and looks out for violator phrases. There's no reason everyone in the family or classroom can't participate.

Week 11—Concision

Purpose: To understand why concise writing is more powerful than bloated writing, and to practice writing concisely.

Here are concise versions of the sentences above:

1. Time everlasting clicks away on the clocks all around us.
Concise: Time passes.

2. It's one of those things that we'll need a real expert to explain to the folks here.
Concise: We'll need an expert.

3. If ever there was a time to get our act together and make some decisions that pertain to this matter, then I'd have to say that time is right about now.
Concise: It's time to make decisions.

4. All hands on deck! Leave no stone unturned! This doesn't have to be a tough nut to crack.
Concise: Let's do it!

5. Many times, a sentence can be a whole lot shorter if you just think hard and maybe get rid of a word or two here or there.
Concise: Sentences can become shorter if you edit.

6. On any given night, when it's dark and everyone's gone for the day, sometimes what I'll do is go into the control room, flick on the lights, and run around the field all by myself, pretending I'm one of the big football stars.
Concise: After everyone's left, I like to turn on the lights and run around the field like a player.

7. Ladies and gentlemen, the time has come to put away any electronic devices that you may be using at this time.
Concise: Put away your electronic devices.

8. So it goes, my friends, this is the way such things go and no one in this entire world can tell me something other than what I saw here with my own eyes just these last past several days.
Concise: I saw it with my own eyes, and no one can tell me differently.

9. Under the hot and scalding rays of the warm sun, the leaves and branches and roots of the tree baked in a painful silence.
Concise: The tree baked in a hot silence.

10. In order to do my homework, I need this book.
Concise: To do my homework, I need this book. (good)
For my homework, I need this book. (better)

Mentor Materials

Section 4: Sound
Weeks 12–17

Week 12—Rhyme

Purpose: To understand the difference between perfect rhymes and near-rhymes and to practice rhyming.

To help the writer, provide him with rhyme pairs and ask what makes a better rhyme: "Tractor" and "actor" or "tractor" and "mentor"? "Tractor" and "factor" or "tractor" and "doctor"? Ask why. Make sure the writer understands that perfect rhymes sometimes make the same sound with not only the final syllable, but the syllable(s) before it, too. Also, make sure that the writer understands that it's not that "actor" is "correct" and "doctor" is "wrong." Simply, they "echo" the word "tractor" in different ways.

Here are some possible rhymes and near-rhymes for the five words in the lesson.

1. hysterical—spherical (perfect), medical (perfect), lyrical (perfect), America (near), generic (near), festering (near)
2. criticize—utilize (perfect), exercise (perfect), ties (perfect), sign (near), side (near), anodyne (near)
3. master—faster (perfect), pastor (perfect), Esther (perfect), taster (near), mast (near), ace (near)
4. intervention—convention (perfect), ascension (perfect), mention (perfect), bastion (near), vent (near), shin (near)
5. salamander—candor (perfect), gander (perfect), stand her (perfect), commando (near), hand (near), candy (near).

I hope you'll find it's a lot of fun digging up rhymes for words!

Week 13—Repetition

Purpose: To continue our study of sound effects in poetry through repetition.

The writer may actually find it easier to write a brand-new poem with an eye toward repetition than to revise something that was originally written with another purpose in mind, and therefore, somewhat difficult to bend to this new goal.

Of course, with a restriction as severe as having to repeat the same word in each line, it's going to be tough for the writer to make perfect sense of her poem, where each line leads into the next in a logical way. Let making sense be a goal, not a requirement.

If the writer can't choose which word to repeat, start from a different direction. Ask the writer what he'd like to write a poem about. If he's stuck, pick a subject you've already used this year, such as the painting poem. Then try to find a fairly common word that might get used a lot in a poem about a painting. How about "brush," or "canvas," or "paint," or—if you're writing about an actual painting—some object in it? A poem that uses the word "brush" at least 10 times can focus on what it was like for the work to be created. A poem that mentions an object inside the painting 10 times can be a riff on the world surrounding that object, like the world the writer had to reconstruct from a photograph in Week 3 of the fiction section. In short, don't start with the word and then force a poem around it. Think of a subject, have the writer make some observations about the subject in his notebook, and then, with key vocabulary in her mind, ask him to pick a word that she thinks he can use at least 10 times. False starts are okay. If something's proving too hard, start over using a different word.

Week 14—Assonance, consonance, alliteration

Purpose: To learn about other sound effects in poetry.

In case the writer gets stuck, here are some sample answers to the exercises in the lesson:

1. Write a sentence that provides at least three examples of **assonance**: On our knees, we scoured the beach for Grandpa's teeth.

2. Do the same for **consonance**: The dragon gave a big roar.

3. Write a minimum five-word sentence where each word begins with the same letter (d): **D**aintily, the **d**ames **d**id **d**ab the **d**ogs' **d**errieres.

4. Write a minimum five-word sentence where each word begins with the letter "b" or "v:" **B**ring the **V**iking **b**oss to the **b**each for a **v**ery **b**ig **b**onanza!

Exercises 6 and 7 feature sample answers.

You can also help the writer by directing him to draw up, in his notebook, a list of words—any words, not necessarily words that make sense in the sentence—that share assonance, consonance, or alliteration with a target word. Freed from the constraint of having to come up with assonant/consonant/alliterative words *and* make sense, they may come up with quite a few that happen to fit the design of the sentence.

Week 15—Sound vs. meaning (Eavesdropping Part II)

Purpose: To learn about how sound works in poetry.

Twenty random lines is a LOT to organize into a poem that tries to make sense. You might help the writer by dividing the lines into "groups" that have something (probably tenuous) in common, meaning-wise. This can force some order on such a large group of lines. Then the writer can "dip" into each group once per stanza, or devote a new stanza to each group.

It's a good exercise as well because it forces the writer to look for connections that may not have to do with meaning. The 20 lines of (eavesdropped) dialogue that she collected are, presumably, fairly random, meaning-wise; so she might rely on other connectors, such as sound. Perhaps two of the lines have words that rhyme. Or perhaps the same words repeat in two lines. (If some of these connections can be helped along by a slight rearrangement of the dialogue line in question, that's fine.) Overall, the goal—even in poem #2, the supposedly more meaning-focused poem—is to get the writer to create a poem where each new line is a bit of a surprise. Both directly and indirectly, this becomes an explicit demonstration of the idea that poetry is about more than the kind of standard, narrative meaning the writer is used to in fiction.

Week 16—A poetic ransom note

Purpose: To understand that poetry is about more than meaning.

Why have the writer try to create a poem that makes sense if the point of the exercise is to appreciate that poetry is about more than meaning? Poetry isn't meant to be nonsense or gibberish. It has an internal logic. It's just that this internal logic is about more than meaning. It's about sound as well—an abstract concept about which the writer will learn a lot more in the next level of this series.

So if the writer starts from a point of complete randomness, but attempts to make sense from it, he's likely to end up with an approximation of what I'm trying to get him to appreciate. It's a roundabout solution to a problem that isn't solvable at this stage of the writer's development, with an instruction like "Write a poem focused on sound rather than meaning." (The logic behind Week 15's exercise is similar.)

Here are the kinds of things you could provide for the writer to cut up and use:
  - Newspapers, magazines, advertisements, circulars, etc.
  - Unneeded packing boxes, cereal boxes, milk cartons, etc.
  - Paper scraps from around the house, such as grocery lists
  - Don't hesitate to practice artistic skills– draw letters, too, as ornately as you'd like!

Week 17—Poem in the shape of...

Purpose: To learn how line breaks influence the look and sound of poetry.

The reading-out-loud portion is a critical part of this exercise. After the writer has read each of the six poems out loud, read them out loud *to* her, taking care to pause at the end of each line. It may be difficult to put into words exactly how the poems differ from each other, but hopefully you'll agree that, indisputably, they do. The exercise is mainly a way of helping the writer see that choosing where to end a line of poetry can have great impact on the sound of the poem. However, it also doubles as a fantastic way to get the writer to come very close to the words of a poem. By the time she's done wrestling these words into five shapes, she will know them almost by heart.

Here's an example of a poem called "The Deserted House," by Alfred, Lord Tennyson, arranged in three different shapes. It's an especially interesting poem to rearrange because it relies so much on rhyme. Our exercise shifts the rhyme to new places, completely changing the echoes of the poem:

Original:

1

Life and Thought have gone away
Side by side,
Leaving door and windows wide:
Careless tenants they!

2

All within is dark as night:
In the windows is no light;
And no murmur at the door,
So frequent on its hinge before.

3

Close the door, the shutters close,
Or thro' the windows we shall see
The nakedness and vacancy
Of the dark deserted house.

4

Come away: no more of mirth
Is here or merry-making sound.
The house was builded of the earth,
And shall fall again to ground.

5

Come away: for Life and Thought
Here no longer dwell;
But in a city glorious—
A great and distant city—have bought

A mansion incorruptible.
Would they could have stayed with us!

As an arrow

Life and
Thought have
gone away Side by
side, Leaving door and
windows wide: Careless tenants
they! All within is dark as night: In the
windows is no light; And no murmur at the door,
So frequent on its hinge before. Close the door, the shutters close, Or thro'
the windows we shall see The nakedness and vacancy Of the dark deserted
house. Come away: no more of mirth Is here or merry-making sound. The
house was builded of the earth, And shall fall again to ground. Come
away: for Life and Thought Here no longer
dwell; But in a city glorious—A great
and distant city have bought A
mansion incorruptible.
Would they could
have stayed
with us!

As a square (or as close as possible)

Life and Thought have gone away Side by side,
Leaving door and windows wide: Careless tenants
they! All within is dark as night: In the windows is
no light; And no murmur at the door, So frequent
on its hinge before. Close the door, the shutters
close, Or thro' the windows we shall see The
nakedness and vacancy Of the dark deserted
house. Come away: no more of mirth Is here or
merry-making sound. The house was builded of
the earth, And shall fall again to ground. Come
away: for Life and Thought Here no longer dwell;
But in a city glorious—A great and distant city
have bought A mansion incorruptible. Would they
could have stayed with us!

Another interesting exercise, suggested by the square, is to render the poem simply as a **piece of prose**, with flush margins. The prose rendering forces the writer to appreciate retroactively just how much the original is a work of sound and not only of meaning.

Life and Thought have gone away Side by side, Leaving door and windows wide: Careless tenants they! All within is dark as night: In the windows is no light; And no murmur at the door, So frequent on its hinge before. Close the door, the shutters close, Or thro' the windows we shall see The nakedness and vacancy Of the dark deserted house. Come away: no more of mirth Is here or merry-making sound. The house was builded of the earth, And shall fall again to ground. Come away: for Life and Thought Here no longer dwell; But in a city glorious—A great and distant city have bought A mansion incorruptible. Would they could have stayed with us!

Mentor Materials

Section 5: Writing a Poem from Scratch

Week 18—Time to write a poem

Purpose: To write a poem from scratch, using all that you've learned this year, but with no restrictions coming from me.

This week, don't correct the writer's work. Let him fly free and explore.